P9-DDF-536

CHRIST IN THE PASSOVER

CHRIST IN THE PASSOVER

WHY IS THIS NIGHT DIFFERENT?

By
CEIL *and* MOISHE ROSEN

MOODY PRESS
CHICAGO

© 1978 by
THE MOODY BIBLE INSTITUTE
OF CHICAGO

Library of Congress Cataloging in Publication Data

Rosen, Ceil.
    Christ in the Passover.

    Bibliography: p. 110.

    Includes index.

    1. Passover. 2. Jesus Christ—Passion. I. Rosen, Moishe, joint author. II. Title.

BM695.P3R67   296.4'37   77-10689

ISBN 0-8024-1392-7

33 35 37 39 40 38 36 34 32 31

Printed in the United States of America

Contents

Preface

"He Who Hath an Ear . . . Let Him Hear"

The Jews are God's chosen people! This is the inescapable teaching of Scripture. Yet that one small statement is enough to disquiet many. No one is more confused by the election of Israel than the Jewish people themselves. To be chosen is a high honor, but how does one live up to it? And some have even wondered: "Why us? If being chosen of God means undergoing the persecutions and suffering that our people have experienced, maybe it would have been better for us if He had chosen someone else!" Nevertheless, God *did* choose *Israel.* He did not choose Israel as a pet people, to be pampered and especially favored; nor did He single her out for persecutions and distress.

Jehovah chose Israel *to teach all nations of Himself,* to witness to the existence of the one true and living God:

> Ye are my witnesses, saith the LORD, and my servant whom I have chosen. . . . I, even I, am the LORD. . . . ye are my witnesses, saith the LORD, that I am God (Isaiah 43: 10-12).

Jehovah chose Israel *to show forth His love and faithfulness:*

> The LORD did not set his love upon you, nor choose you, because ye were more in number, . . . for ye were the fewest of all people: but because the LORD loved you, and

7

because he would keep the oath which he had sworn unto your fathers (Deuteronomy 7:7-8).

Jehovah chose Israel *to be a blessing to all people* through the seed of Abraham:

> Now the Lᴏʀᴅ had said unto Abram, . . . I will make of thee a great nation, and I will bless thee . . . and thou shalt be a blessing . . . and in thee shall all families of the earth be blessed (Genesis 12:1-3).

Jehovah chose Israel *to be a praise to Him:*

> This people have I formed for myself; they shall shew forth my praise (Isaiah 43:21).

Jehovah chose Israel *to bring forth salvation to all mankind:*

> Ye worship ye know not what: we know what we worship: for salvation is of the Jews (John 4:22).

Through Israel came the holy writings, the promises of God, and the Redeemer. Sometimes Israel was an unwilling teacher; at times Israel strayed. But God used even the lapses of faith, even the disobedience, as object lessons to those who wanted to learn of Him. Like Jonah of old, the chosen people will serve God in one way or another. The joy of serving Him comes only with the relationship born of obedience. But willingly or unwillingly, Israel shall serve the Lord!

All that befell ancient Israel has a direct bearing on God's people today. The apostle Paul wrote in 1 Corinthians 10:11: "Now all these things happened unto them [Israel] for ensamples [by way of example]: and they are written for our admonition."

Everything the people of the Bible were, everything they

did, both as a nation and as individuals, can be a lesson to
us today. Through the history of His people, Israel, we see
the hand of the Almighty guiding, directing, showing what
He expects of His people. Israel's customs and traditions
are more than just quaint folkways to be studied by histori-
ans and anthropologists. Her history is a memorial of the
past and a guidepost to the future.

In the saga of His special people, Israel, God shows to all
mankind:

1. The unsatisfactory condition of the natural human
   heart
2. His willingness to forgive and restore
3. The way He has provided that all people might come
   to Him
4. The faithfulness and constancy of His love

From the loins of faithful Abraham, God formed this
special people. He called Abraham out of paganism and
idolatry and established his seed as a great nation to be an
example to the heathen. He gave His special people a
Law and a land. He commanded them to keep the Sabbath
as a reminder of creation and their Creator, and He ordained seven religious feasts to be observed every year
(Leviticus 23:5-44). First, Israel had to learn from her
own history to know and trust the one true God. Then His
dealings with the Jewish people were to be a beacon to
steer all the nations away from idolatry and sin to saving
faith in their Creator.

Events and teachings in Scripture often have more than
one meaning. There is the obvious contemporary event to
which there can be one or more prophetic counterparts,
and there can also be a spiritual application. The ancient
feasts of Jehovah, which He gave to Israel, cast the shadow

of a greater future reality. There was a threefold aspect to those annual festivals: first, the seasonal celebration based on the agrarian culture of that time; second, the historical remembrance of God's dealings with the nation; and third, a future fulfillment.

Even as God orders the universe and commands the seasons of nature, so He has ordained times and seasons to bring about His order and plan of salvation for the human race. Israel's feasts of Jehovah portray the stages of God's dealings with man, which will culminate in the completion of that plan.

Feast	Season	Temporal Significance for Israel Under the Law	Future Significance For All God's People Under Grace	Scripture	Event
PASSOVER	Spring (new beginning)	Redemption from bondage in Egypt	Believers in Christ redeemed from bondage of sin	"Ye were not redeemed with corruptible things, as silver and gold, . . . but with the precious blood of Christ, as of a lamb without blemish and without spot" (1 Peter 1:18-19).	THE CRUCIFIXION (Redemption)
UNLEAVENED BREAD	Spring (new life)	Purging of all leaven (symbol of sin)	All believers in Christ cleansed from sin and empowered to walk in newness of life	"Purge out . . . the old leaven, that ye may be a new lump. . . . For even Christ our passover is sacrificed for us" (1 Corinthians 5:7).	(Sanctification)
				"[God] made him to be sin for us, who knew no sin; that we might be made the righteousness of God in him" (2 Corinthians 5:21).	(Justification)
FIRSTFRUITS	Spring (first of grain harvest)	Thanksgiving for firstfruits, the promise of the harvest to come (first of the grain presented to God)	Christ, the First to rise from the dead—the promise of resurrection and eternal life for all who believe on Him	"But now is Christ risen from the dead, . . . the firstfruits of them that slept. . . . even so in Christ shall all be made alive" (1 Corinthians 15:20-22b).	THE RESURRECTION OF CHRIST
FEAST OF WEEKS (Pentecost)	Late spring seven weeks after Passover (ingathering of first harvest)	Thanksgiving for first harvest and	God's first harvest of those redeemed in Christ (Jews and Gentiles)	"And when the day of Pentecost was fully come, . . . they were all filled with the Holy Ghost. The same day there were added unto them about three thousand souls" (Acts 2:1-4, 41b).	THE COMING OF THE HOLY SPIRIT and
		(according to oral tradition, the time of the giving of the Law at Sinai)	God's Law written on the hearts of the redeemed	"I will put my laws into their hearts, and in their minds will I write them" (Hebrews 10:16).	THE BIRTH OF THE CHURCH

(SUMMER, A TIME OF LABOR IN THE FIELDS AND PREPARATION FOR FINAL HARVEST—THE CHURCH AGE)

"Lift up your eyes, and look on the fields; for they are white already to harvest" (John 4:35).

Feast	Season	Temporal Significance for Israel Under the Law	Future Significance For All God's People Under Grace	Scripture	Event
FEAST OF TRUMPETS	Early autumn	A solemn assembly (trumpets blown to prepare for the Day of Atonement)	The beginning of the regathering of Israel to the land in preparation for the final Day of Atonement	"I will gather them out of all countries, whither I have driven them, . . . and I will bring them again unto . this . place, and I will cause them to dwell safely" (Jeremiah 32:37).	ISRAEL REGATHERED
			The assembly of all believers, dead and alive, in the heavens with Christ	"For the Lord himself shall descend from heaven with a shout, with the voice of the archangel, and with the trump of God: and the dead in Christ shall rise first: then we . . . . shall be caught up together . . . to meet the Lord" (I Thessalonians 4:16-17; 1 Corinthians 15:52).	THE RAPTURE OF THE CHURCH and THE RETURN OF CHRIST
DAY OF ATONEMENT	Autumn	A solemn assembly for repentance and forgiveness under the Law (repeated annually)	Believers in Christ forgiven by one atonement for all time	"So Christ was once offered to bear the sins of many" (Hebrews 9:28).	
			The rest of Israel will repent and look to her Messiah	"And I will pour upon the house of David, and upon the inhabitants of Jerusalem, the spirit of grace and of supplications: and they shall look on me whom they have pierced, and they shall mourn for him. In that day there shall be a fountain opened to the house of David and . . . Jerusalem for sin and for uncleanness" (Zechariah 12:10, 13:1).	ISRAEL TURNS TO HER MESSIAH
FEAST OF BOOTHS	Autumn (final harvest)	Harvest celebration and memorial of tabernacles in the wilderness	Joyous assembly— all peoples brought under the rule of the King Messiah	"Every one that is left of all the nations which came against Jerusalem shall even go up from year to year to worship the King, the Lord of hosts, and to keep the feast of tabernacles" (Zechariah 14:16).	THE KINGDOM OF GOD ON EARTH

1

Why Passover?

When Abraham, the first Hebrew, left Ur of the Chaldees to follow the call of the living God, he sacrificed a life of comfort and ease. Ur was no village. It was one of the oldest, most important cities of Mesopotamia, covering an area of about four square miles by the Euphrates River, which empties into the Persian Gulf. The citizens of Ur, numbering well over half a million, lived in walled safety. They enjoyed the advantages of the highest culture and civilization of their time. They took particular pride in the outstanding architecture of their temples, which they built in honor of their numerous deities, and in the fact that their city was the center of worship for the popular moon-god religion.

From the comfort, advantages, and sophistication of Ur, Jehovah called Abraham and his family to a seminomadic way of life. They were not nomads in spirit, for they had God's promise of the land; but, in fact, they did not possess it. They wandered with the seasons, seeking pasture for their flocks, but they also tilled the ground. Tents were their only shelter from the scorching sun and cruel desert wind, but they buried their dead in permanent caves, an act of faith that showed they believed that one day the land really would be theirs. They trusted God for future stability and a permanent home, but they knew it was not yet time.

Then a great drought and famine drove Jacob, a grandson of Abraham, to leave Canaan for the promise of food in Egypt. Once again the seed of Abraham dismantled their tents. Packing all that they had acquired and their scant remaining food and water supply, they headed south with their wives, their little ones, and their flocks. For Joseph's sake, Pharaoh welcomed Jacob and his sons as honored guests, laying Egypt's resources at their feet and giving them the land of Goshen for their dwelling place (Genesis 47:6). Goshen was a fertile area along the delta of the Nile River, lying in the northeast portion of an area between what is now Cairo to the southeast and Alexandria to the northwest. Here the Hebrews felt respected and secure.

Egypt Is Our Home—Why Bother About Canaan?

Because of the devastating drought that drove Jacob to seek refuge in Egypt, most of the Egyptians were starving also. Many sold their cattle, their land, and finally themselves to Pharaoh in exchange for food. But Jacob's sons flourished and prospered. Because the pharaohs of that time were of Semitic descent, they favored the seed of Abraham, who also were Semites. For the first time since Abraham left Ur, the Hebrews enjoyed a feeling of permanence. They lived a quiet, secure, pastoral life in Goshen. The Nile overflowed its banks once a year, bringing life-giving water to the earth. There was lush, abundant pasture for the flocks, and rich soil to grow their food.

Here the Hebrews watched their children grow tall and brown in the sun. At night they slept in safety, with no desert wind howling through the solid walls of their adobe homes. No longer did they awake to the distressed bleating of hungry flocks, a signal that once again they must

move on. Their Egyptian neighbors were people of high morals and advanced culture. Not only did they produce literature and music, but they also knew mathematics and a degree of the healing arts, and many were skilled architects. They accepted the Hebrews as equals and even bestowed high honors on some of them. Life was pleasant indeed.

In this situation the descendants of Abraham prospered for hundreds of years. Exodus 1:9 indicates that they multiplied so fast that a later pharaoh grew concerned that there were more Hebrews than Egyptians in the land. The children of Israel were so comfortable and secure that it was easy to forget that Egypt was not the land God had promised to their fathers. Maybe some of them even forgot God Himself.

O Lord, Forgive Our Complacency—Get Us Out of Here!

For the seed of Abraham, Egypt had been a volcano threatening to erupt. For more than four hundred years they lived at the edge of that volcano without knowing it. Now the volcano erupted and its flames threatened to consume them, for there arose a new pharaoh who "knew not Joseph" (Exodus 1:9). Fearing the strength and power of the vast multitude of Hebrew foreigners, he turned against them and made them his serfs. The children of Israel continued to live in Goshen, but the land no longer belonged to them. Now they belonged to the land, to Egypt, and to the pharaoh, who *was* Egypt. They had to serve him with backbreaking labor, sweating in the fields, building his treasure cities, without recompense or even dignity. There were no problems with labor relations, no labor-management arbitrations. Pharoah owned everything and every-

one. He appointed taskmasters, foremen to make sure that the proper amount of work was done. When Pharaoh decided to oppress the Hebrews, he simply ordered the taskmasters to give them more work than they could do. Life was cheap in Egypt. If a man dropped from exhaustion, the taskmasters left him to die and quickly whipped another into line to take his place.

Under the cruel pharaoh, the children of Israel toiled and suffered, but still they grew in numbers. Enraged, Pharaoh ordered the Hebrews' male babies murdered so that the entire nation would eventually die. Then the Israelites remembered the God of their fathers. At last they recognized their need to be rescued. They needed to be delivered, not only from Pharaoh, but from Egypt itself. They cried out to God in their bondage and distress, and He heard their anguished pleas. Now that they were ready for His help, He remembered His covenant with Abraham, with Isaac, and with Jacob. Deliverance was near.

Egypt to the Hebrews had become comfort and complacency outside God's providence. The covenant Jehovah made with Abraham was two-sided. On God's part, He promised the land (Genesis 15:18); on Abraham's part, he and his seed were to bear the physical marks of the covenant—circumcision (Genesis 17:10). The Hebrews did remember to circumcise while they were in Egypt (Joshua 5:5), but they prevented God from fulfilling the covenant by not seeking the land He had promised. They broke the spirit of the covenant. They needed to be redeemed, to be "deemed again" the people of the covenant, the people of God.

Jehovah could have slain the wicked pharaoh in an instant to alleviate the sufferings of His people. He could have brought about a new, more favorable order in Egypt.

But that would not have been enough. The sons of Jacob had to forsake Egypt in order to serve the living God. Old things, old attitudes, old affections had to pass away—all things had to become new. The Bible teaches that a person cannot see the Kingdom of God until he is spiritually born again (John 3:3). So the nation of Israel also needed a new beginning, a new birth. Thus the redemption at Passover prepared the sons of Jacob for another covenant to be made at Sinai, which would reestablish and reaffirm them as the nation of God.

The Passover redemption from Egypt changed Israel's reckoning of time.° God commanded the Hebrews to count the month of the deliverance from Egypt as the first month of the year. He was saying, in effect, "This event is so historic that you are to rearrange your calendar because of it." They were to count their existence as a people from the month of Nisan. (Even so, we of modern time mark our history B.C. and A.D., basing our calendar on Calvary, the pivot point of God's dealings with humanity through the Messiah.) And thus, with this new beginning to occur shortly, Israel, the great nation that God had promised to its father, Abraham, was about to become reality.

°By tradition, the Jewish people celebrate the fiscal New Year in the fall, in the seventh month of the Jewish calendar; but the religious calendar begins in Nisan, the first month.

2

The Egyptian Passover

In order to carry out His plan to redeem His people from Egypt, Jehovah chose a man who was, in many ways, as much an Egyptian as he was a Hebrew. Moses was born an Israelite. The blood of Abraham flowed in his veins, but he grew to manhood in the palace of Pharaoh's daughter. As an infant he was raised by his Hebrew mother, but he learned worldly wisdom from Egyptian schoolmasters. God chose him to deliver Israel, to show to all that "the LORD doth put a difference between the Egyptians and Israel" (Exodus 11:7b).

As a young man, Moses fled Egypt in disgrace under penalty of death. When God called him to lead Israel out of bondage, he had been away from Egypt's culture and sophistication for forty years. Long ago he had given up his princely robes for the rough garb of a shepherd. Now he stood before the successor to the pharaoh who had sought his life. His eyes blazed from his weather-beaten face with the fire of the living God, whom he had encountered in the wilderness. His hand, calloused by the shepherd's crook, wielded a miraculous staff. His lips formed the syllables of the holy NAME as he confronted Pharaoh with the words of the Lord: "Let my people go!"

When Pharaoh refused, the Lord demonstrated His might by bringing down judgment on Egypt's false gods.

Through Moses, He turned the waters into blood, showing His power over the Nile, which the Egyptians worshiped as the sustainer of life. He darkened the sky, proclaiming His superiority over the sun-god, Ra. He made pests of the frogs, which the Egyptians respected as controllers of the undesirable insects that followed the annual overflow of the great river.

The Lord poured out plague after plague; still Pharaoh hardened his heart. God ruined the Egyptians' crops with hail and locusts, killed their cattle with disease, and afflicted the people with painful boils, loathsome vermin, and thick darkness. Calamities threatened Egypt's prosperity on every side, but the Israelites were spared. Pharaoh hardened his heart even further, however, and now the cup of iniquity was full. God had said to Pharaoh through Moses: "Israel is my son. . . . Let my son go, that he may serve me; and if thou refuse, . . . I will slay thy son, even thy firstborn" (Exodus 4:22-23). Now He determined to break the iron will of Egypt with one last plague. The specter of death was to fly by night over the land, breaking the cycle of life, interrupting the line of inheritance, bringing tragedy to every home where Jehovah was not feared and obeyed.

Although their redemption was at the door, the Israelites were not automatically exempt from this last plague. God tempered His final judgment on Egypt with mercy and perfect provision—the substitution of a life for a life.

> In the tenth day of this month they shall take to them every man a lamb, . . . a lamb for an house, . . . and ye shall keep it up until the fourteenth day of the same month: and. . . . kill it. . . . And . . . take of the blood, and strike it on the two side posts and on the upper door post of the houses. For I will pass through the land of Egypt

. . . and will smite all the firstborn. . . . And the blood
shall be to you for a token upon the houses, . . . and when
I see the blood, I will pass over you, and the plague shall
not be upon you (Exodus 12:3-7, 12-13).

The verb "pass over" has a deeper meaning here than
the idea of stepping or leaping over something to avoid
contact. It is not the common Hebrew verb, *a-bhar*, or *ga-bhar*, which is frequently used in that sense. The word
used here is *pasaḥ*, from which comes the noun *pesaḥ*,
which is translated *Passover*. These words have no connection with any other Hebrew word, but they do resemble
the Egyptian word *pesh*, which means "to spread wings
over" in order to protect. Arthur W. Pink, in his book
Gleanings in Exodus, sheds further light on this. Quoting
from Urquhart, he states:

> "The word is used . . . in this sense in Isa. 31:5: 'As birds
> flying, so will the Lord of Hosts *defend* Jerusalem; defend-
> ing also He will deliver it; and passing over (pasoach, par-
> ticiple of pasach) He will *preserve* it'. The word has, con-
> sequently, the very meaning of the Egyptian term for
> 'spreading the wings over', and 'protecting'; and *pesach*,
> the Lord's Passover, means such sheltering and protec-
> tion as is found under the outstretched wings of the Al-
> mighty. Does this not give a new fulness to those words
> . . . 'O Jerusalem! Jerusalem!. . . . How often would I
> have gathered thy children together, as a hen does gather
> her brood under her wings' (Luke 13:34)? . . . this term
> *pesach* is applied (1) to the ceremony . . . and (2) to the
> lamb. . . . The slain lamb, the sheltering behind its blood
> and the eating of its flesh, constituted the *pesach*, the pro-
> tection of God's chosen people beneath the sheltering
> wings of the Almighty". . . . It was not merely that the
> Lord passed by the houses of the Israelites, but that He

stood on guard, *protecting* each blood-sprinkled door!
["The LORD . . . will not suffer the destroyer to come in"
(Exodus 12:23*b*).]*

God includes everyone in the death sentence in Exodus
11:5: "All the firstborn in the land of Egypt shall die."
God must do the right thing because He is God, but He
balances His righteousness with His loving mercy. He
decrees judgment for all sin and all sinners; then He provides a way of escape, a *kiporah* or covering. When the
rain falls from above, it falls on everyone. But those who
have an umbrella do not become wet. For those who
seek His way to satisfy the demands of His Law, God provides an umbrella of safety. In His judgment of Egypt,
He provided the umbrella of the blood of the Passover
lamb.

Israel's redemption began that night behind the sanc-
tuary of those blood-sprinkled doors. It was a night of
horror and grief for anyone who had foolishly disregarded
God's command; it was a long, dark night of awesome vigil
mixed with hope for the obedient. Perhaps they heard
wails of anguish from outside as the grim reaper went
from house to house; perhaps there was only thick, omi-
nous silence. They knew that terror and death lay outside
that door, which they dared not open until morning. But
within was safety.

It was a night of judgment, but the substitutionary death
of the Passover lamb brought forgiveness to God's people,
Israel. It washed away 430 years of Egypt's contamina-
tion. The blood of the lamb protected them from the
wrath of the Almighty. Its roasted flesh nourished their
bodies with strength for the long, perilous journey ahead.
They ate in haste, loins girded, staff in hand, shoes on their

*Arthur W. Pink, *Gleanings in Exodus*, p. 93.

feet, prepared to leave at any moment at God's command. In that awe-filled night of waiting, they experienced Jehovah's loving protection, even in the midst of the unleashing of His fierce judgment. They learned new trust, a trust that was deep enough to see them through another black night soon to come. They would stand at the edge of the churning waves of the Red Sea with the entire host of angry Egyptians at their backs, and they would trust the words of Moses: "Stand still, and see the salvation of the LORD" (Exodus 14:13).

The Lord often works on behalf of His people when things look darkest. In the words of the psalmist, "Weeping may endure for a night, but joy cometh in the morning" (Psalm 30:5). And so the morning came, and with it abounding joy and freedom.

Thus, out of His mercy, and because He would keep His covenant with the fathers, the Lord rescued Israel. It was a new birth, a new beginning. This time the seed of Abraham must not forget their commitment to the Holy One of Israel; they must not forget His promises. They must remember that He brought them out of Egypt with a strong hand and with His outstretched arm.†

---

†A word study on the "Arm of the Lord" is particularly significant in view of idiomatic use in connection with the rescue from Egypt.

3

Passover, God's Object Lesson

The Lord's redemption of Israel needed to be stamped indelibly on the minds and hearts of future generations. He intended that the ancient experience should have a lasting effect on His people; its importance must be reinforced with regularity for all time.

Yet how can a people best remember its history? Books and scrolls capture only the interest of the scholarly; in time, words lose their meaning. God, the master Teacher, devised the perfect method. He commanded the annual re-enactment of that first Passover night, a ceremony that would appeal through the senses to each person of every generation. Even as we teach little children today through object lessons, Jehovah took everyday acts of seeing, hearing, smelling, tasting, and touching and made them His allies in teaching holy truths to His people.

THE LAMB

God began His object lesson to Israel with the Passover lamb. First, the people had to single out from their flocks the handsomest, healthiest looking yearling. An animal of this age, just approaching the prime of its life, was frisky and winsome. Then the family had to watch it carefully for four days before the Passover to make sure it was healthy and perfect in every way. During this period of

25

close observation, they fed and cared for the lamb and
grew accustomed to having it around the house. By the end
of the fourth day, it must have won the affection of the
entire household, especially the children. Now they all
must avoid its big, innocent eyes as the head of the house
prepared to plunge in the knife to draw its life's blood.
They did not have meat very often in ancient times, but
how could they enjoy eating the lamb's flesh? The lesson
was painfully sad: God's holiness demands that He judge
sin, and the price is costly indeed. But He is also merciful
and provides a way of escape (redemption).

The innocent Passover lamb foreshadowed the One who
would come centuries later to be God's final means of
atonement and redemption. The parallels are striking.

THE PASSOVER LAMB WAS MARKED OUT FOR DEATH

In Isaiah 53:7 is the prophecy that the Messiah will be
led as a lamb to the slaughter; 1 Peter 1:19-20 says Jesus
was foreordained to die before the foundation of the world.

THEY WATCHED THE PASSOVER LAMB TO SEE THAT IT WAS
   PERFECT

According to Deuteronomy 15:21, only that which is
perfect can make atonement. Jesus the Messiah presented
Himself to Israel in public ministry for three years and
showed Himself perfect in heart and deed toward the
Father. Even Pilate found no fault in Him. Hebrews 4:15
says that He was tempted (tested) in all points, yet was
without sin; 1 Peter 1:19 describes Him as a Lamb without blemish or spot.

THEY ROASTED THE PASSOVER LAMB WITH FIRE

Fire in Scripture speaks of God's judgment. Isaiah the

prophet foretold that the Messiah would bear the sins of many, be wounded for sins not His own, be stricken with God's judgment, and be numbered with transgressors. As Jesus the Messiah suffered the fire of God's wrath and judgment, He cried out from the cross: "My God, my God, why hast thou forsaken me?" (Matthew 27:46). Second Corinthians 5:21 says: "He [God] hath made him [Christ] to be sin for us . . . that we might be made the righteousness of God in him."

NOT A BONE OF THE PASSOVER LAMB WAS BROKEN

The Roman soldiers did not break the legs of Jesus the Messiah as they did the legs of the other two men crucified beside Him.

Redemption through the death of the Passover lamb was personal as well as national. Even so, salvation must be a personal event. In Exodus 12:3, the commandment is to take *a* lamb, a nebulous, unknown entity, nothing special; in Exodus 12:4, God says "the" lamb. Now he is known, unique, set apart. Finally, in Exodus 12:5, God specifies, "*your*" lamb; each redeemed soul must appropriate the lamb for himself. Arthur Pink quotes Galatians 2:20 to apply this truth to faith in the Messiah: "The life which I now live in the flesh I live by the faith of the Son of God [the Messiah], who loved *me,* and gave himself for *me.*"*

The New Testament refers to Jesus the Messiah more than thirty times as the Lamb of God. Faith and trust in the sacrifice of God's Lamb make a person or a nation belong to God. Exodus 12:41 calls the people of Israel the "hosts of the LORD," not the hosts of Israel. Redeemed by the blood of the Passover lamb, they truly belonged then to God.

*Arthur W. Pink, *Gleanings in Exodus,* pp. 89-90.

The Bitter Herbs

With bitter herbs they shall eat it (Exodus 12:8).

Jehovah commanded the Israelites to eat the Passover lamb with bitter herbs. The first symbolism that comes to mind is the obvious one—the hardships which the Israelites endured under the whips of Pharaoh's taskmasters. But there is a deeper lesson as well. Bitterness in Scripture often speaks of death. The bitter herbs are a reminder that the firstborn children of the people of Israel lived because the Passover lambs died. God created man to gain life through death, to receive physical sustenance from the death of something that once was alive, be it plant or animal. Even so, the believer in the Messiah Jesus receives new life through His death as the Lamb of God.

Bitterness in Scripture also speaks of mourning. Zechariah 12:10 prophesies that one day Israel as a nation will weep and be in bitterness of deepest mourning for her Messiah, as when one mourns for an only child who has died. God says in Zechariah 13:9 that He will bring Israel through the judgment of fire and refine her even as silver and gold are refined. Then Israel will proclaim, "The Lord is my God," and in that day "the Lord shall be king over all the earth" (Zechariah 14:9).

The Unleavened Bread

And they shall eat the flesh in that night, roast with fire, and unleavened bread (Exodus 12:8).

The next symbol in God's object lesson is the unleavened bread. The children of Israel ate the Passover lamb with bitter herbs and unleavened bread; then they were to eat no leaven for a full seven days afterward. The lesson went deeper than the obvious haste of the departure from Egypt.

Leaven in the Bible is almost always a symbol of sin.†
The putting away of all leaven is a picture of the sanctification of the child of God. Cleansed, redeemed by God's
lamb, the true believer must put away the sinful leaven
of the old life before redemption.

In teaching His people this truth, God did not leave
them to grapple with abstractions. The Bible speaks in
terms of human experience. Leaven was something that
every housewife, every cook, used in everyday life. The
feel, the smell, the effects of leaven had obvious meaning.

The Hebrew word for leaven is *chometz,* meaning "bitter" or "sour." It is the nature of sin to make people bitter
or sour. Leaven causes dough to become puffed up so that
the end product is more in volume, but not more in weight.
The sin of pride causes people to be puffed up, to think
of themselves as far more than they really are.

The ancient Hebrews used the sourdough method of
leavening their bread. Before the housewife formed the
dough into loaves ready for baking, she pulled off a chunk
of the raw dough and set it aside in a cool, moist place.
When it was time to bake another batch of bread, she
brought out the reserved lump of dough. She then mixed
the old lump into the fresh batch of flour and water to
leaven the next loaves, again setting aside a small lump
of the newly mixed dough. Each "new generation" of
bread was organically linked by the common yeast spores
to the previous loaves of bread. The human race bears
this same kind of link to the sin nature of our first father,
Adam.

Often people excuse themselves for bad behavior or
wrong attitudes by saying, "I'm only human." But being

†Once, in Matthew 13:33, it is used as a symbol of growth and expan-
sion.

"only human" is the sin nature within all mankind. Jesus spoke of leaven as false doctine and hypocrisy (Matthew 16:11-12; Mark 8:15; Luke 12:1, 13:21).

The apostle Paul, in 1 Corinthians 5:6-8, spoke of leaven as pride, malice, and wickedness. He said, "Purge out therefore the old leaven, that you may be a new lump [a new person] as ye are unleavened [cleansed]. For even Christ our passover is sacrificed for us."

On the other hand, Paul described the *un*leavened bread as sincerity and truth. The Hebrew word *matzo* (unleavened) means "sweet, without sourness." The unleavened bread typified the sweetness and wholesomeness of life without sin. It foreshadowed the sinless, perfect life of the Messiah, who would come to fulfill all righteousness and to lay down His life as God's ultimate Passover Lamb. In Passover observances after the cessation of the Temple sacrifices, the *matzo* (unleavened bread) took on added significance when the rabbis decreed it to be a memorial of the Passover lamb.

Thus, for the Hebrews, the putting away of all leaven symbolized breaking the old cycle of sin and starting out afresh from Egypt to walk as a new nation before the Lord. They did not put away leaven *in order* to be redeemed; rather, they put away leaven *because* they were redeemed. This same principle applies to the redeemed of the Lord of all the ages. Salvation is of grace, "not of works, lest any man should boast" (see Ephesians 2:8-9).

THE BLOOD ON THE DOOR

And ye shall take a bunch of hyssop, and dip it in the blood that is in the bason, and strike the lintel and the two side posts with the blood that is in the bason; and

none of you shall go out at the door of his house until the
morning (Exodus 12:22).

Several times Scripture mentions a special mark that
will secure immunity from destruction for those who fear
the Lord. One such text is Ezekiel 9:4-6; two others are
found in Revelation 7:2-3 and 9:4.

When Egypt's judgment was imminent, God commanded the sons of Israel to mark the doors of their dwell-
ings with the blood of the Passover lamb. Those marks
painted on the doors set apart the houses of those who believed and obeyed God from the houses of those who did
not.

The "bason" mentioned in Exodus 12:22 was not a container in the sense in which we use the word *basin* today.
The word is the Egyptian *sap*, meaning the threshold or
ditch which was dug just in front of the doorways of the
houses to avoid flooding. The people placed a container
in the ditch to prevent seepage. The Israelites killed their
Passover lambs right by the doors, where they were about
to sprinkle the blood, and the blood from the slaughter
automatically ran into the depression (the bason) at the
threshold. When they painted the blood on with the
hyssop "brush," they first touched the lintel (the top hori-
zontal part of the doorframe), then each side post (the
vertical sides.) In doing this, they went through the mo-
tions of making the sign of a bloody cross, the prophecy
of another Passover sacrifice to come centuries later. Thus,
the door was "sealed" on all four sides with the blood of
the lamb, because the blood was already on the bottom.
Author Pink sees this as a picture of the suffering Messiah
Himself: "Blood above where the thorns pierced His

brow, blood at the sides, from His nail pierced hands;
blood below, from His nail pierced feet."‡

We see further symbolism in the words of Jesus, when
he said: "I am the door: by me if any man enter in, he shall
be saved, and shall go in and out, and find pasture" (John
10:9). The Israelites went in through the blood-sealed
door on that first Passover night and found safety. Protected and redeemed by the sacrificial blood, they went
out the next morning and began their journey toward the
good pasture, the land of promise. We who are redeemed
by the true Passover Lamb find safety in Him from God's
judgment, and, because of Him, we look forward to a
future, eternal haven in the very presence of the Almighty,
in the city whose "builder and maker is God" (Hebrews
11:10).

‡Pink, p. 93.

4

A Night to Be Much Observed

Delivered from the plague of death by the blood of the Passover lamb, the children of Israel greeted the dawn of their redemption with new trust born of experience. The night before, they were timid slaves cowering behind locked doors. Now they threw open their doors and windows to the morning sun and rejoiced in their deliverance. Awed by the power of the Almighty that had protected them from the death angel, they were ready to follow Moses, His servant.

That very morning, the Egyptians, fearful of Jehovah's further wrath, begged the Hebrews to leave the country immediately. There was no time to prepare food for the journey. The Israelites bound up their unleavened dough, still in the kneading bowls, and strapped it to their backs. With this meager supply of food, they set out from Egypt with their wives, their little ones, their aged, their flocks, and all they possessed. They left nothing behind, and their beasts of burden were weighed down with the riches pressed upon them by their frightened Egyptian neighbors.

Four hundred and thirty years earlier, seventy people had come into the land of the pharaohs with Jacob. This day a mighty throng, the hosts of Jehovah, went out. The Bible records that six hundred thousand men left Egypt. Their mothers, wives, and children surely swelled their

numbers to almost two million. This newly formed nation
would wander in the desert for forty years. A whole generation would grow old and die before they entered
Canaan, the land that flowed with the milk of goats and
the honey of figs. But they relied on God's promise that
it would come to pass, and they already had His instructions.

> And this day shall be unto you for a memorial; and ye
> shall keep it a feast to the LORD throughout your genera-
> tions; ye shall keep it a feast by an ordinance for ever
> (Exodus 12:14).

> And it shall come to pass, when ye be come to the land
> which the LORD will give you, according as he hath prom-
> ised, that ye shall keep this service. And . . . when your
> children shall say unto you, What mean ye by this service?
> That ye shall say, It is the sacrifice of the LORD's passover,
> who passed over the houses of the children of Israel in
> Egypt, when he smote the Egyptians, and delivered our
> houses (Exodus 12:25-27).

> It is a night to be much observed . . . of all the children of
> Israel in their generations (Exodus 12:42).

> And thou shalt shew thy son in that day, saying, This is
> done because of that which the LORD did unto *me* when *I*
> came forth out of Egypt* (Exodus 13:8, italics added).

The word "observed" used in Exodus 12:42 comes from
the Hebrew root *shamar*, which means "watch." Even as
the Lord kept watch over the blood-protected homes of
the children of Israel on that first Passover, they, in turn,
were to keep watch on each annual Passover night of remembrance. It was to be a memorial forever.

---

*Each Jewish person, for all time, must consider himself, personally,
one whom the Lord delivered from bondage.

To the early Hebrew fathers, a memorial was more than a grave marker or a milestone to indicate time or space. They used the memorial to bring to mind or authenticate important events. Throughout the book of Genesis, Abraham, Isaac, and Jacob built altars or placed markers at the sites where God had appeared to them. These markers stood as reminders of God's promises to the seed of Abraham: to make of them a great nation; to give them a land; to make them a blessing to all people.

Now God commanded the annual memorial of the Passover observance so that His people might reflect regularly upon all that He had done for them. When they would come into the promised land and partake of its goodness, they were to remember the Lord. They were to rehearse and retell the events of the great redemption He had wrought for their fathers. They were to rejoice in His past and present blessings, and look forward to what He would yet do for and through them.

God gave specific regulations for this celebration of the anniversary of redemption.

1. All the congregation of Israel must keep the Passover (Exodus 12:47).
2. They must not allow any stranger to eat the Passover, that is, no one who was uncircumcised or outside the covenant (Exodus 12:43-45).
3. They must eat the Passover in one house, that is, a lamb for a household. The household could be more than one family, as long as they came together under one roof (Exodus 12:46).
4. They must eat the Passover sacrifice entirely in one night, not leaving any for the morning (Exodus 34:25).

5. They must put away all leaven from their tables and from their houses for seven days (Exodus 13:6-7).
6. They must offer the blood of the sacrifice without leaven (Exodus 34:25).
7. They must not break any bones of the Passover lamb (Exodus 12:46).
8. They must sacrifice the Passover only at the place appointed by God (Deuteronomy 16:5-6).
9. All the males of the congregation must appear before the Lord at Passover time (Exodus 23:17, 34:23).

Only those who were of the household of faith could participate in the Passover festival of redemption. If Gentile visitors or servants wanted to share in the memorial, they first had to become Jews, that is, undergo circumcision, which would make them part of the covenant. The fulfillment of God's promise to Abraham, that in his seed (the Messiah) all the nations of the earth would be blessed, has done away with that kind of restriction. Now all those who trust in Israel's Messiah for redemption belong to the new covenant of grace. They have undergone circumcision of the heart (Jeremiah 31:31-33) and are eligible to celebrate the new memorial. As Paul wrote to the Ephesian believers, the Gentiles, who at one time were "aliens from the commonwealth of Israel, and strangers from the covenants of promise," are now by faith in Jesus, the Lamb of God, "no more strangers and foreigners, but fellow-citizens with . . . the household of God" (Ephesians 2:12, 19).

But now the problem is reversed. As Israel celebrated the memorial of redemption from Egypt, now there is an even greater redemption to commemorate: forgiveness of sin and new life through Jesus, God's perfect Lamb. Now

God's people only in the flesh must submit to circumcision of the heart and be brought under the new covenant in order to have a part in the memorial of that greater redemption.

After those instructions concerning Passover at the time of the Exodus, the Scriptures record only one actual observance during the forty years of the wilderness journey. Numbers 9:1-14 describes a Passover celebration on the fourteenth day of the first month in the second year after the departure from Egypt, "according to all that the LORD commanded Moses" (v. 5). At that time God made provision through Moses for a second or "minor Passover," as rabbinical commentaries later called it. Anyone who was ceremonially unclean or who had been away on a journey on the fourteenth day of the first month, the regularly appointed time, could instead celebrate the Passover on the fourteenth day of the second month.

No other Passover celebration is recorded in the Bible until we read of the children of Israel's coming into the land of Canaan. This lapse was probably due to the problem of circumcision. Joshua 5:5 seems to indicate that they suspended the law regarding circumcision during the wilderness journeys, possibly because of the dangers of infection. Then, as the older generation died in the desert, no one was left who had been circumcised, and no one was eligible to carry out the Passover memorial.

In Joshua 5:7-9, the first thing that the Lord commanded Joshua when the Hebrews came into the land was the circumcision of all the males who had been born in the wilderness. Thus, the Lord "rolled away the reproach of Egypt" (v. 9), and the children of Israel kept the Passover on the fourteenth day of the month in their new homeland.

Second Kings 23:22 records that after Joshua's death, from the time of the Judges until the time of the several reforms in the kingdom of Judah, there had not been such a great Passover observance. The people, who once had heard God's thundering voice from the holy mountain, had listened to the voice of temptation and had fallen into idolatry. Passover was undoubtedly observed during the time of Samuel and in the reigns of David and Solomon, and occasionally after the united kingdom divided; on the whole, however, the Word of God was not in the Israelites during most of that period, so they were not seeking to follow God's commandments concerning Passover or anything else. But then their hearts were stirred by revival.

The writer of 2 Chronicles tells of two such revivals and the Passover celebrations that immediately followed. One happened in the reign of King Hezekiah (726 B.C.), and the other during the reign of King Josiah (621 B.C.).

Second Chronicles 30 records the Passover of Hezekiah. The king ordered the priests and Levites to cleanse and rededicate the Temple and to sanctify the altar. He sent letters to all the people in Israel, Judah, Ephraim, and Manasseh to come up to the house of the Lord in Jerusalem to celebrate the Passover. As a result, a great revival took place, and the people kept the Feast of Unleavened Bread with much gladness and singing. So great was their joy that they kept the feast for an additional seven days after the first seven. The Scriptures say there was not such great joy in Jerusalem since the days of Solomon; the Lord heeded their prayers and healed their backsliding.

Second Chronicles 35:1-17 tells of the Passover celebration after reform and revival under King Josiah. Verse 18 of this chapter records the fact that there had been no Passover celebration of this magnitude since the days of Samuel

the prophet, "neither did all the kings of Israel keep such a passover."

Then, in 586 B.C., the king of Babylon destroyed the Temple and carried the people away into exile. In Babylon, the children of Israel were once again strangers in a foreign land. Perhaps their circumstances reminded them of their ancestors' bondage in Egypt. But if this prompted them to keep the Passover, we have no record of how they observed it.

Further scriptural mention of the Passover is in Ezra 6:19. After the return from Babylon, the Israelites rebuilt the Temple and "the children of the captivity kept the passover upon the fourteenth day of the first month."

At that time, not all the Jewish people returned to the land. Some stayed in Babylon, where they had built businesses and made new lives for themselves; others migrated and formed small Jewish communities throughout the civilized world. Ancient records bear out the fact that in those days the exiles observed Passover as a permanent part of Jewish religious life. They could not sacrifice the Passover lamb unless they made a pilgrimage to Jerusalem, but they did keep the other two important precepts of the holiday: they purged all leaven from their households, and they ate unleavened bread for seven days.

Thus, throughout the history of the children of Israel, the Passover celebration, or the neglect of it, stood out as a thermometer indicating the Jewish community's spiritual condition. Under the rule of the kings, decadence from within affected the people's religious commitment. In the intertestamental period (c. 400 B.C. to A.D. 50), persecution and oppression by their Gentile conquerors spurred the Jewish people to renewed spiritual fervor, for they esteemed most highly what they were in danger of losing.

For the next historical mention of the Passover, one must look to the noncanonical writings of the intertestamental period. The Book of Jubilees (second century B.C.) speaks of the offering of the Paschal lamb at Jerusalem. It emphasizes both the formal procedures and the expressions of praise and joy of the Passover festival of that period. Pilgrimages were made to Jerusalem to keep the Passover, and other appointed feasts of Jehovah played an important role in Jewish religious life.

As time went on, each learned rabbi, and each succeeding generation of his disciples, added customs and traditions to embellish the Passover celebration. Nevertheless, the underlying theme always remained the same: the Almighty had brought freedom and new life to His people, Israel, through His supernatural power.

The memory of that miracle-filled redemption occupied the people's minds and hearts at Passover. The tangible, visible symbol of that memorial was the solemn sacrifice of the Paschal lamb at the Temple in Jerusalem. As the Jews celebrated Passover during those years of uncertainty and change, hope ran high that soon the Messiah would come to vanquish the Roman oppressor, even as the Lord had brought deliverance from the wicked pharaoh in days of old.

5

Passover in the Time of Christ

At Passover, a constant stream of humanity ribboned the highways leading into first-century Jerusalem. Devout Jews poured in from distant corners of the world to worship Jehovah in the mountain of His holiness. If at all possible, those Jews who lived within a few days' journey came up to Jerusalem three times a year: at Passover, at Pentecost, and at the Feast of Booths. But for many who lived very far from Jerusalem, the lengthy pilgrimage at Passover was the fulfillment of a once-in-a-lifetime dream.

Weeks before the holiday, the trickles began—from Asia Minor, from Egypt, from Africa, from Italy, from Greece, from Mesopotamia*—and soon the stream became a river. The current of this river flowed upward. Whether the first part of the journey was by boat or by land, no one ever went *down* to Jerusalem.† The holy city sat like a crown 2,610 feet above sea level, and the Temple was its brightest, most prominent jewel. In order to reach this destination, all travelers first had to go through the surrounding valleys. The contrasting loftiness of that final ascent built a sense of holiness and awe within the pilgrims as they climbed ever upward.

By mule, in ox cart, on foot they came: families, schools

*See Acts 2:9-11.
†Even in modern times the Hebrew word used for visiting Jerusalem is *Aliyah,* which means "going up."

41

of disciples following their teachers, solitary travelers banded together in caravans for safety from robbers and wild animals. As they drew near, their joyful voices rang out and echoed through the valleys below in the Pilgrim Psalms or Songs of Ascent:

> As the hart panteth after the water brooks, so panteth my soul after thee, O God (Psalm 42:1).

> How amiable are thy tabernacles, O LORD of hosts! My soul longeth . . . for the courts of the LORD (Psalm 84:1-2).

> I was glad when they said unto me, Let us go into the house of the LORD. Our feet shall stand within thy gates, O Jerusalem (Psalm 122:1-2).

> Behold, how good and how pleasant it is for brethren to dwell together in unity! (Psalm 133:1).

> Behold, bless ye the LORD . . . ye servants . . . which by night stand in the house of the LORD (Psalm 134:1).

The number of permanent residents in the Jerusalem that Jesus knew was about six hundred thousand. A conservative estimate of the vast multitude of Passover pilgrims is about two million, who swelled the city's population to almost four times its normal size. Those who came from afar arrived at least a week or two in advance, because anyone coming from a country outside of Israel could not worship in the Temple before undergoing seven days of ritual purification.

At Passover, Jerusalemites and their visitors, despite vastly differing cultural backgrounds, rejoiced in the unity of their Jewishness. It was a time for renewal of family ties. People were reunited with blood kin whom they had not seen for months or even years. Pilgrims without relatives or friends at Jerusalem found themselves being wel-

comed as family members into homes where they had never been, by people they had never met.

The earliest to arrive camped around the Temple site, as the tribes had once camped around the tabernacle in the wilderness, but this space was limited. The area surrounding Jerusalem was too rocky and hilly for pitching large numbers of tents, so all residents who were able opened their homes to the visiting worshipers. They were forbidden by custom to charge rent, but it was a joyful obligation. Almost every home had guests. Jerusalemites often entertained exotic visitors who had tales to tell of distant places and different cultures. Usually the host and his household were given hospitality gifts, exciting things that brought the sight, smell, and feeling of adventure.

During the four weeks before Passover, the synagogues and academies placed much emphasis on teaching and reinforcing the holiday's meaning. Jerusalem was filled with excitement and expectancy, and all the citizenry prepared for the festivities and the influx of visitors. Members of the Sanhedrin busied themselves with arrangements for the repair of roads and bridges leading into the city. Housewives scrubbed and polished, and they sewed new garments for everyone in the household. Vendors in the marketplaces expanded their stock in eager anticipation of increased business. Even the beggars, huddling at the gates in their rags, dreamed of a season of bounteous compassion and generosity, prompted by the worshipers' piety.

One preparation custom involved whitewashing the tombs around the city. The people of that time buried their dead in caves and sealed off the openings with large stones, so that wild animals would not desecrate the bodies. But the numerous caves around Jerusalem were used for other purposes as well. People kept livestock in

caves,‡ and also used them for shelter. It was possible that
a traveler, seeking refuge at night or during a spring rain-
storm, might blunder into a burial site. Since this contact
with a dead body would defile him, he would have to undergo an elaborate ritual cleansing before being able to
worship in the Temple. For this reason, they marked the
tomb entrances and surrounding areas with a white, chalky
material to warn people. This whitewash wore off and
needed replacing periodically, and it was the custom to
do these repairs at the Passover season.

These freshly painted tombs provided Jesus with the
imagery He used to rebuke the Pharisees in Matthew 23:
27-28. They thought of themselves as a repository of truth
and light, but there was an infectious spirit of death to
their self-righteousness. Their outward piety looked good
and right, but men were to be warned away from their
teachings, because following them would only lead to
death and decay.

Jerusalem was a commercial city as well as the seat of
government and religion. The most common meeting
grounds to befriend strangers and offer them hospitality
were the gates of the city, the marketplaces, and the synagogues.

The Jerusalem of Jesus' time had about three hundred
sixty synagogues. The city was small enough geograph-
ically not to need neighborhood divisions. Rather, the con-
gregations consisted of people with like interests, like
trades, and like stations in life. Thus, there were synagogues of potters, synagogues of tentmakers, synagogues of
Greek-speaking Jews, and so forth.

The synagogue was not only a place of learning. It

‡Such a stable at Bethlehem sheltered Mary and Joseph at the birth
of Jesus.

took the place of the community center, the grange, the hiring hall, the fraternal lodge. Here people in the trades met their foreign counterparts and exchanged knowledge, and artisans were introduced to new methods and designs. Passover was a time for seeking new apprentices, and those who came early for the holiday might join the craftsmen in their trades.

In the marketplaces, the tables and blankets of wares held a larger than usual and more colorful variety of goods. Many of the travelers brought trade goods to be used for currency; food producers supplied extra commodities, often of a more luxurious nature than their everyday products, to meet the increased needs and festive mood. Here was a rare spice, an exotic ointment; there, a delicate piece of woven material, a familiar homespun made intriguingly different by the startling brilliance of some new dye, a new kind of carpenter's tool, a cleverly designed potter's wheel, a finely crafted silver wine goblet, or an elaborately concocted food to tease the nostrils.

At Passover, Jerusalem was filled with itinerant rabbis and teachers, who often brought along their whole academies. These scholars enriched the homes of their hosts with the benefit of their knowledge and inspiration. All rabbis were learned in matters of the Law, and at this time they had the opportunity to compare notes and share interpretations and precedents of both Jewish and Roman law.

It was a time for making business deals, and a time for servants who had made the decision to undergo the ritual which would indenture them for life to their masters' households. It was a time for those of the priestly class to renew their acquaintance with Temple customs; their sons might have an opportunity to sing with the Levitical choir,

or they might find a bride of equal station. It was a matter of prestige to marry a daughter of Jerusalem, for those women were not of peasant stock and often came from priestly, scholarly, or merchant families. In general, it was a time for seeking wives and for arranging marriages.

Passover season was an ideal time to sit in the market-place or at the gates and enjoy the skillful art of conversation. Jewish people of that time usually did not play physical games for recreation and entertainment, as did the Greeks and Romans. Rather, they delighted in songs, storytelling, word games, riddles, the exchange of news, and long discussions on religious matters. In those crowded public places, one could hear interesting bits of news. Sometimes they were merely entertaining, other times rather useful. One might learn of battles, of uprisings, of scandals among rulers, of a particularly lenient tax collector at one of the tollgates, or of a wealthy merchant seeking a son-in-law.

Jerusalem was a beehive of activity. Crowds thronged the streets, their voices blending with the lowing of cattle and the bleating of sheep and goats. Vendors hawked their wares; people shouted greetings to one another. There was a good-natured air of festivity. Then, amid the bustle and din, a change in the wind might carry down the sound of the Temple services—the music, the chanting of the priests. People then turned their eyes upward to the towering structure high atop Mount Moriah, which dominated the landscape in all directions. They saw the smoke from the sacrifices curling upward against the sky, and they remembered their real purpose for being there: the worship of Jehovah, the true and living God. That was the scene; those were the sights, the sounds, the smells

that greeted Jesus and the disciples as they entered Jerusalem the week before the Passover.

A crucial part of the final preparations that last week before the feast was the removal or storing away of all leaven in each Jewish home. That included bread, all leavening agents, and any cereals or grains that had the capacity of becoming leavened. There was also the ceremonial cleansing of the pots and utensils in the house.

On the night before Passover eve, a search was made for any leaven that might have been overlooked. At that time, the head of the household went through the house, inspecting it with a lighted candle or lantern in complete silence. If he found any leaven, he disposed of it or locked it away where it would not be touched until after the Passover and the eight days of unleavened bread, which followed. Then the head of the house repeated an ancient prayer, which Orthodox Jews still use today: "All leaven that is in my possession, that which I have seen and that which I have not seen, be it null, be it accounted as the dust of the earth."

Alfred Edersheim wrote of this search: "Jewish tradition sees a reference to [this] searching out of the leaven in Zephaniah 1:12."§ Speaking of judgment, God said in that verse: "I will search out Jerusalem with candles," meaning He will search out the leaven of sin and destroy it. The apostle Paul probably had this search for the leaven in mind when he said in 1 Corinthians 5:7: "Purge out therefore the old leaven [sin], that ye may be a new lump, as ye are unleavened [cleansed from sin]. For even Christ our passover is sacrificed for us."

§Alfred Edersheim, *The Temple, Its Ministry and Services as They Were at the Time of Jesus Christ*, p. 220.

At the same time that people throughout the city were preparing their homes, special attention was being given to the central subject of the feast, the Paschal lamb. In obedience to Scripture, a representative of each household chose the sacrifice lamb on the tenth of Nisan. If someone bought a lamb outside the Temple, he had to bring it to be inspected by the priests and declared without blemish or spot; or he could buy a lamb already certified by the priests within the Temple complex. Most people bought lambs in the Temple, knowing from bitter experience that the priests could almost always manage to find some minute imperfection on any animal brought from the outside.||

On the fourteenth of Nisan, the slaughter of the Passover lambs took place. The priests chose "companies" of not less than ten people, nor more than twenty. Each group sacrificed one lamb, which they later ate as their ceremonial meal. The crowds of worshipers entered by company into the Temple's outer courtyard. The Levites killed the lambs at the signal of the silver trumpets sounded by the priests. Then they removed the fat and burned it. They caught the blood of the sacrifices in bowls, which two rows of priests passed along to be poured out at the base of the altar.

While all this was happening, the Levitical choir chanted Hallel, the recitation of Psalms 113 to 118. The congregation joined in the liturgy by repeating the first line of each psalm after the Levites sang it. They also chanted the words *Hallelu Yah* (praise ye the Lord) at the end of every line. When the priests came to Psalm 118, the congregation repeated verses 25 and 26:

||This is why Jesus cried out in anger: "Ye have made it [the house of God] a den of thieves" (Matthew 21:13; cf. Mark 11:15-17; Luke 19:45-46).

> Save now, I beseech thee, O LORD [*Hoshia Na,* or Ho-
> sanna]
> O LORD, I beseech thee, send now prosperity.
> Blessed be he that cometh in the name of the LORD.

These are the very words that rang out through the streets
of Jerusalem a week before the crucifixion as Jesus rode
into the city on a donkey in fulfillment of Zechariah 9:9.
The two disciples sent by Jesus to prepare the Passover
heard them again as they stood in the court of the priests
to kill their lamb. As their memory of that joyful acclaim
mingled with the reality of the death scene before them,
one wonders whether they began to understand what the
Master had been trying to tell them when He said:

> Behold, we go up to Jerusalem, and all things that are
> written by the prophets concerning the Son of man shall
> be accomplished. For he shall be delivered unto the Gen-
> tiles, and shall be mocked, and spitefully entreated, and
> spitted on: and they shall scourge him and put him to
> death (Luke 18:31-33; cf. Matthew 20:18-19, 26:2; Mark
> 9:31-32, 10:33-34).

6

The Ancient Seder and the Last Supper

THE ANCIENT SEDER

The Pharisees of Jesus' day regarded the oral traditions of the ancient sages as being of equal authority with the Torah, the written law of God. Orthodox Jews today still believe that God Himself delivered these oral traditions to Moses, and that they were then passed by word of mouth to each succeeding generation. Those earliest known rabbinical commentaries were edited and compiled into one authoritative body of religious thought called the Mishnah sometime between A.D. 100 and 210. The Mishnah covers every aspect of Jewish religious life and presents a picture of the customs, traditions, and observances at the time of Christ.

According to the Mishnah, the basic obligations of the Passover observance are the same as those commanded in the book of Exodus. In Pesaḥim 10:5, the Mishnah quotes Rabbi Gamaliel as saying:

> Whoever does not make mention of the following three things on Passover has not fulfilled his obligation; namely, the Passover sacrifice, unleavened bread and bitter herbs. The Passover sacrifice because the Holy One . . . passed over the houses of our fathers in Egypt; unleavened bread

. . . because our fathers were redeemed from Egypt; the bitter herb . . . because the Egyptians embittered the lives of our fathers in Egypt.

By the first century, the Passover observance included several new customs in addition to the obligations described in the Torah account. Already, a set form of service called the *seder*, meaning "order of service," was in use. The celebrants reclined at the table in the Babylonian custom of free men. (Slaves stood in attendance while their masters ate.) The ceremony included ritual hand washings and set prayers. The celebrants drank four cups of wine as a symbol of joy. Oral tradition contained in the Mishnah commanded that even the poorest person must drink the minimum four cups, even if he had to sell himself to do labor or had to borrow money in order to buy the wine. The Passover wine was red and mixed with water. From a passage in the Mishnah (Pesahim 7:13), it would appear that the wine was warm because the water was heated. If this is true, then the wine graphically represented the blood of the Passover lamb, as well as being a symbol of joy.

Beside the roasted Paschal lamb, the bitter herbs, and the unleavened bread,* other ceremonial foods were on the table. Salt water or vinegar was used for dipping the bitter herbs once. Then there was *charoseth,* a sweet mixture of apples and nuts. Into this mixture they dipped the bitter herbs and the unleavened bread together. They ate no dessert or after dish; for, after eating the Passover lamb, no other solid food was to be taken. The after dish, known as the *aphikomen,* came into use later, after the destruction

---

*Some sources indicate there were two flat cakes of unleavened bread; others say there were three.

of the Temple in A.D. 70. It was a wafer of the unleavened
bread, representing the Paschal sacrifice, which was no
longer possible.

We will consider contemporary Passover customs and interpretations later, but let us visualize here how the Passover ritual was observed in the time of Christ.

At the outset, the head of the feast (the host) recited
kiddush over the first cup of wine. This prayer consecrated
the occasion and the meal to God. The words, if not exactly
those used today, were very similar.

> Blessed art Thou, O Lord our God, who hast created the
> fruit of the vine. . . . Blessed art Thou, O Lord our God,
> who hast sustained us and enabled us to reach this season.

Next came the ceremonial *washing of hands* by the host.
At this point a servant brought in a portable table of food,
and the *first dipping* of food took place. This was the raw
vegetable, usually lettuce, which was considered a bitter
herb. The head of the feast dipped the vegetable into salt
water or vinegar and passed it around to all at the table. It
was a common practice for beginning a meal, and it can be
likened to hors d'oeuvres or appetizers. But here, as in all
things that were eaten and done on that night, there is a
deeper symbolism, which is discussed later.

After the dipping of the bitter herb, the food was removed from the table. Then the host poured the *second
cup* of wine, but the participants did not drink it yet. Re-
moving the food without eating the main course (the
Paschal lamb) was an unusual procedure intended to raise
curiosity.

The next step in the ritual would then follow naturally.
This was the asking of questions by the youngest son so

they could obey the command of God, "Thou shalt shew thy son."†

The questions in ancient times were:

> Why is this night different from all other nights? On all other nights we eat leavened or unleavened bread, but this night only unleavened bread.
>
> On all other nights we eat all kinds of herbs, but this night only bitter herbs. Why do we dip herbs twice?
>
> On all other nights we eat meat roasted, stewed, or boiled, but on this night why only roasted meat?

Then the father gave a synopsis of Israel's national history, beginning with the call of Abraham out of idolatry and ending with Israel's deliverance from Egypt and the giving of the Law. After that, the food was brought back. The father continued the service by explaining the lamb, the bitter herbs, and the unleavened bread. Then they sang the first part of the Hallel (Psalms 113 and 114) and *drank the second cup* of wine.

They then *washed hands* the second time, as an act of respect for the unleavened bread they were about to eat. The host broke one of the wafers and pronounced the *blessings over bread.* There were two blessings. One was a prayer of thanksgiving to Him who brings forth bread from the earth; the second was thanksgiving for the commandment to eat unleavened bread. Traditionally, these blessings were spoken over bread that had first been broken in order to show humility, remembering that the poor had only broken bits of bread to eat. The host gave a piece of this broken bread, dipped in bitter herbs and the sweet charoseth mixture, to each person.

†The command to expound on the story of redemption is mentioned three times—Exodus 10:2, 12:26-27, and 13:8.

After the bitter herbs and the bread, they ate the Paschal lamb. If the lamb was too small for everyone to have enough, they also ate the *Haggigah* (a holiday peace offering). But, in that case, they ate the *Haggigah* first, so that the Passover lamb would be the last food they ate that night. Then, of course, there was no dessert.

After supper, the host poured the *third cup* of wine and they all recited the blessing after meals. Then they chanted another special blessing for wine over the third cup, and everyone drank it.

After the third cup, they recited the second portion of the Hallel (Psalms 115-118) and drank the *fourth cup*. The seder came to an end with a *closing song* or *hymn*, which began: "All thy works shall praise Thee, Jehovah, our God," and concluded: "From everlasting to everlasting Thou art God, and beside Thee, we have no King, Redeemer or Savior."

THE ANCIENT SEDER AND THE LAST SUPPER

The Passover ordinance commemorated Israel's historical redemption from Egyptian slavery. God gave it as an object lesson to be observed by all those who counted themselves as being made free by His power. But equally important was the hidden symbolism of a greater, future redemption, which one day would free all those who cried out to God in their sin and despair—a redemption for all people, Jews and Gentiles, to bring them into a new and eternal relationship with their Creator and with each other —the redemption through King Messiah. The Jewish people yearned and prayed for that redemption as they groaned under the yoke of Rome. Yet when the fulfillment of the promise was at the door, few recognized it.

The Teacher from Nazareth came into their midst, exciting the masses with His words of wisdom spoken with authority. He healed the sick, opened the eyes of the blind, caused the lame to walk, and showed miraculous power over the physical laws of nature. Many hoped that He was the One to free the nation from its oppressors and set up God's Kingdom on earth, but they expected Him to do it by military might. Expectation ran high as Jesus entered Jerusalem that last week before the Passover. By tradition, many of the important events of Israel's history had taken place at Passover season; even as He had redeemed Israel from Egypt at the Passover season and had given her His holy Law, so God was to send the Messiah at Passover.

The faithful and the scoffers watched Jesus carefully those few days before the Passover. They saw Him overthrow the money tables in the Temple. What would He do next? Would He tell them that He, indeed, was the long-awaited Messiah? Alas, they were disappointed. He only continued to teach, and many of the things He said were not comforting to hear.

Now it was the eve of the Passover celebration. Jesus sent two of the disciples, Peter and John, to prepare for the ritual meal. They found a room as He had instructed them and performed all the necessary preliminaries. All was in readiness. Jesus reclined with the twelve at the Passover table to take His last meal with them. Here, on the eve of His death, He showed them the full meaning and symbolism of the Passover memorial.

The picture of that Last Supper comes into sharper focus when the account of Scripture is compared with the ancient order of the Passover service:

THE KIDDUSH:

> And he took the cup, and gave thanks, and said, Take this,
> and divide it among yourselves: for I say unto you, I will
> not drink of the fruit of the vine, until the kingdom of God
> shall come (Luke 22:17-18).

THE FIRST WASHING OF HANDS:

> He riseth from supper, and laid aside his garments; and
> took a towel, and girded himself . . . and began to wash
> the disciples' feet (John 13:4-5).

(Table of food brought; bitter herbs dipped in salt water;
table of food removed; second cup of wine poured; ritual
questions asked; ritual answer given; table of food brought
back; explanation of lamb, bitter herbs, and unleavened
bread; first part of Hallel; second cup taken; second washing of hands; one wafer of bread broken; and thanks over
bread recited.)

BROKEN PIECES OF BREAD DIPPED IN BITTER HERBS
AND CHAROSETH, AND HANDED TO ALL:

> And when he had dipped the sop, he gave it to Judas
> Iscariot, the son of Simon (John 13:26).
> Then said Jesus unto him, That thou doest, do quickly.
> He then having received the sop went immediately out
> (John 13:27b, 30a).

(The Paschal meal eaten; hands washed a third time;
third cup poured.)

BLESSING AFTER MEALS:

> Jesus the same night in which he was betrayed took
> bread: and when he had given thanks, he brake it, and
> said, Take, eat: this is my body, which is broken for you:
> this do in remembrance of me (1 Corinthians 11:23-24).

BLESSING OVER THIRD CUP (CUP OF REDEMPTION):
> After the same manner also he took the cup, when he had
> supped, saying, This cup is the new testament in my
> blood: this do ye, as oft as ye drink it, in remembrance of
> me (1 Corinthians 11:25).

(Third cup taken; second part of Hallel recited; fourth
cup poured and taken.)

CLOSING SONG OR HYMN:
> And when they had sung an hymn, they went out into the
> mount of Olives (Matthew 26:30).

The first hand washing by the host set him apart from
the rest of the company. It showed that he was the most
important person at the table. In washing the disciples'
feet, Jesus used this part of the regular ritual to teach His
lesson of humility and love. He acted out the role of a slave
when He girded Himself with the towel and washed their
feet. He knew that the Father had given Him all things;
even the wind and the sea obeyed Him. Yet He humbled
Himself. He taught them that it was not the ceremonial
rite, but the act born of faith and love, that was important.
And so He took upon Himself the most humiliating task
and truly loved them *all* to the end. He even washed the
feet of Judas!

It was during the ceremony of dipping the second sop
into the bitter herbs that Jesus said, "One of you shall be-
tray me" (Matthew 26:21). Peter motioned to John, who
was reclining so that he leaned on Jesus' bosom, to ask who
the betrayer was. Jesus whispered His answer: "He it is,
to whom I shall give a sop" (John 13:26).

One may wonder why John did nothing to stop Judas.
But it must be remembered that the statement could have

been taken to mean any one of them at the table. They all partook of the sop, although Judas probably received it first. After the sop, Judas went out into the night to finish his Satan-inspired work. Because he left before eating the Passover, he had, in effect, excommunicated himself from the congregation. Neither did he have any part in the new memorial that came after supper.

The bread that Jesus broke for the bitter sop was not the bread of which He said, "This is my body" (Matthew 26:26*b*). That came later. We see this from the account that He took that bread *after* He first gave thanks at the end of the meal; *then* He broke it and gave it to them, saying, "This is my body which is given for you: this do in remembrance of me" (Luke 22:19; cf. 1 Corinthians 11:24).

Not only the words were shocking. It was a very unusual act, for after supper no other food was to be eaten. Jesus here instituted the new memorial. He was teaching the disciples in cryptic terms that after His death, the Paschal lamb would no longer have the same significance. It was the memorial of physical, historical redemption, but only a shadow of the ultimate redemption soon to come. He was about to become the better sacrifice, to die once, for all (Hebrews 9:14-15, 23-26). Looking to the time when Israel would be left without an altar and without a sacrifice, He used the *aphikomen* (after dish) for the first time to represent not only the Paschal lamb, but His own body!

And then He took up the wine again and prepared the third cup for them: "Likewise also the cup after supper, saying, This cup is the new testament in my blood, which is shed for you" (Luke 22:20). He who was the great "I AM" come in the flesh had stood before them on other occasions saying, "I am the way, the truth, and the life" (John 14:6); "I am the door" (10:9); "I am the light of the world"

(8:12); "Before Abraham was, I am" (8:58). Now He had one more great truth to impart to those who could receive it. He was telling them, in effect: "I am the true Passover Lamb who will be offered up for your redemption. This warm, red wine, which you drink tonight as a symbol of joy, is to remind you evermore of My life's blood, which will be poured out as an atonement for you!"

The gospel accounts of the Last Supper mention only two of the four seder cups—the first and the third. According to early Jewish tradition, these two were the most important. The first cup was special because it consecrated the entire Passover ritual that followed. But the Mishnah states that the third cup was the most significant of all. The third cup had two names: the "cup of blessing," because it came after the blessing or grace after meals, and the "cup of redemption," because it represented the blood of the Paschal lamb. It was of *this* cup that Jesus said, "This is my blood of the new testament [covenant]" (Matthew 26:28). It is *this* cup of blessing that Paul mentions in 1 Corinthians 10:16: "The cup of blessing which we bless, is it not the communion of the blood of Christ? The bread which we break, is it not the communion of the body of Christ?"

PASSOVER AND EASTER

Almost all the early Christians were Jewish. They celebrated the resurrection of Jesus at Passover time and called it *Pascha*. (Later it was mistranslated Easter.) They continued to celebrate the resurrection in this manner during the time of the first fifteen bishops of Jerusalem, who were of Jewish descent.‡ The bishops sent out Paschal epistles every year to notify the Christians when Pascha would fall

‡Epiphanius *Panarion Haer.* 70.10; Eusebius *Eccles. Hist.* 5.23.

according to the Jewish lunar calendar (i.e., the fourteenth
day of Nisan). By A.D. 325, however, paganism and anti-
Jewish sentiment had invaded the Church; Emperor Con-
stantine, who presided over the Council at Nicaea, pro-
hibited Christians from continuing to celebrate the resurrection at exactly the same time as the Jewish Passover.§
Still, to this day, the two holidays are celebrated at ap-
proximately the same time, both being based on the lunar
calendar.

The death and resurrection of Jesus the Messiah are forever interwoven with the Passover and its symbolism. The
Passover lamb spoke of the Lamb of God who was to come;
the redemption from Egypt spoke of the greater redemption that the greater Lamb would bring. To deny these
truths of Scripture is not only to miss a rich heritage, but
to cut oneself off from God. A believer who would purpose
to do so is like the man who climbs a tree and then tries to
chop it down while seated in its branches!

Some well-meaning, albeit misinformed, Christians today have accused Jewish Christians of "Judaizing" and
"Galatianism" because they choose to celebrate Jewish holidays and remember their cultural roots. Nothing is further
from reality. The Jewish believer in Jesus finds deeper
significance and reinforced faith in seeing God's commandments and the customs of His people, Israel, in the new
light of salvation in Christ. These things are relevant to our
faith, not in opposition to it. We gain no merit with God
in observing the festivals; but if we ignore them, we miss
the blessings of a deeper appreciation of the heritage that is
the cradle of our faith and subsequent salvation.

The apostle Paul dealt with this subject when he wrote
by the moving of the Holy Spirit in Romans 14:5-6a, 10,

§Solomon Zeitlin, *The Jewish Quarterly Review* 28, no. 4 (April 1948).

> One man esteemeth one day above another: another esteemeth every day alike. Let every man be fully persuaded in his own mind. He that regardeth the day regardeth it unto the Lord; and he that regardeth not the day, to the Lord he doth not regard it. But why dost thou judge thy brother? or why dost thou set at nought thy brother? for we shall all stand before the judgment seat of Christ.

And again, he wrote in Colossians 2:16-17:

> Let no man therefore judge you in meat, or in drink, or in respect of an holyday, or of the new moon, or of the sabbath days: which are a shadow of things to come; but the body is of Christ.

Contemporary seder plate with six symbolic foods (coun-
terclockwise from bottom): chazereth, baytzah, karpas,
maror, charoseth, and zeroah. (See pp. 68-69.)

7

The Contemporary Passover

As long as the second Temple stood, Jerusalem remained the hub of Jewish life. Then, in A.D. 70, Roman legions leveled the great house of worship. The prophetic words of Jesus became history, its pages written in blood and stained with tears.* Only rubble and ashes—painful reminders of past splendor—covered the Temple site.

Exiled, without an altar and without a sacrifice, the Jewish people felt a deep need to remember and rehearse the great things Jehovah had done for them in days past. They clung to the hope that once again He might do marvelous things for His people.

It is fitting that this hope should continue to burn in the hearts of God's chosen people, for "the gifts and calling of God are without repentance" (Romans 11:29). Against all odds, through centuries of oppression and struggle, the Jewish people survived. They nurtured the memories of the past and fervently looked for a future deliverance. Each Jewish family, each small community, bore the responsibility of keeping a spark of faith alive in the darkness and despair of exile. The holidays and traditions—links in the chain of survival—became more important than ever. So the celebration of "The Season of Our Deliverance" took on new meaning and a new setting.

---

*"There shall not be left one stone upon another, that shall not be thrown down" (Matthew 24:2; Mark 13:2; Luke 21:5-6).

The people of the Diaspora embellished and added to the required ritual of the Passover in order to intensify and reinforce the holiday's meaning. They wrote special songs so the ear might have melodies and rhythms to remind the heart; celebrants reclined on cushions to promote a sense of freedom and relaxation; they used lamps and candles to give a greater measure of brightness so they could see the festival's familiar elements in a new light. Even the sense of taste was involved as they adopted new foods from new cultures to enhance the holiday table with unique and savory dishes. They continued to drink the four cups of wine to symbolize gladness. Still, the main course of the feast was conspicuously missing!

What can Passover be without the Passover lamb? It is like a birthday party complete with cake and candles for a departed loved one, or like a wedding without the bride. The holiday that Jewish people today call Passover is really the eve of the Feast of Unleavened Bread. The remembrance of redemption from death by the blood of the lamb is overshadowed by emphasis on the redemption from Egyptian slavery and thoughts of national liberty. Nevertheless, we still call the holiday Passover. Although this is not entirely accurate, there is good precedent for using the title. Even as far back as Bible times, the two observances—Passover and the Feast of Unleavened Bread—were referred to by both names, and they were often treated as one holiday.†

How, then, do Jewish people celebrate Passover today? We shall not find the answer in the synagogue. It is not in the pages of the well-worn prayer books; nor is it in the parchment scrolls of Holy Writ encased in their mantles of

†Matthew 26:17; Mark 14:12; Luke 22:1. Josephus once called it "A feast for eight days" (*Antiquities* 2. 15.1; cf. 3.10. 5 and 9. 13. 3).

scarlet and blue velvet, embroidered with gold and silver thread. The first Passover ritual took place in individual homes. There they were, Hebrew families gathered around the table for a meal—a meal that was to become the epic symbol of past redemption and future hope. So we must look again into the home, the family unit, to see and know the Passover of today.

THE PREPARATION

The Jewish housewife tackles her spring cleaning with a holy zeal! This is because Passover comes in the spring, in the month of Nisan, also called Abib. She is preparing to obey the command in Exodus 12:19: "Seven days shall there be no leaven found in your houses." Do the walls need paint, carpets need shampooing, cupboards need rearranging? Wait until just before Passover! The straw broom of ancient days has given way to the vacuum cleaner; and instead of the city dump, we have garbage disposals. The means may be different, but the end result is still the same. Every scrap of bread, every cookie crumb, every bit of yeast, every speck of baking powder or other leavening agent must go. The housewife must also banish from the home all grain products that have the capability of becoming leavened. If she has too many of these costly staples to throw away, the rabbis have provided a remedy. She stores all the items in one place in the house. This can be a high, out-of-the-way shelf or, better yet, an unused room. Then she finds a Gentile friend, who is not bound by the laws of Israel, to buy title to all the leaven. The purchase price is a token amount, usually a dollar or two. Now, technically, the leaven is no longer in the possession of the Jewish householder, though it remains locked away in the house. After the seven days of the holiday, the Gen-

tile friend will sell back all the leaven (for the same low price, one would hope!).

Now it is the thirteenth of Nisan, the day before the Passover celebration. The house is hospital clean. Even the floors gleam and sparkle. The rays of the late afternoon sun stream in through windows so spotless they look invisible. Not in any corner, nor under any piece of furniture, is there so much as a speck of dust or a crumb of leaven. But the house is not yet "clean."

As in ancient times, the ceremonial search for the leaven, called *Bedikat Chametz*, must follow. The ceremony and the prayer remain much the same as they were two thousand years ago, and the man of the house gets the credit for all the backbreaking work. Some rabbinical authorities command that he must search every room; others say only those rooms that would normally have food in them.

For the search, the head of the house takes with him a child, to hold the lighted candle, and some strange cleaning equipment—a wooden spoon, a feather, and an old cloth napkin. He searches upstairs and downstairs, in the attic, in the basement, and in all the rooms until he comes to the last room. The housewife knows beforehand which room this will be. Just so he will not have said the prescribed prayer in vain, she has placed a few crumbs in a highly visible spot where he can find them easily. They may be the crumbs from his morning toast, but now they are something unclean! He points the feather at the offending material and sweeps it into the wooden spoon. Then he wraps spoon, feather, and crumbs in the old napkin and pronounces the words of the ancient formula: "Now I have rid my house of leaven."‡ The next morning he joins the other men of the Jewish community at a desig-

‡This prayer is called the *Kal Hamira*. Cf. chap. 5, p. 47.

nated ritual bonfire. They all toss in their bundles of leaven and return home ready for the Passover.

After the house is ritually clean, the housewife puts away the everyday dishes and brings out special dishes that are used only at Passover. If the home is too poor to afford special dishes, the old dishes must be ritually cleansed. This is a complicated process. The rule is that the metal utensils like pots and pans must be heated until red hot; cutlery must be placed in boiling water; glazed ware must be soaked in cold water. Because unglazed pottery is too porous and cannot be cleansed, it must be put away until after the holiday.

THE SEDER TABLE

At sundown on the fourteenth of Nisan, everything is in readiness for the beginning of the festivities. The children are as scrubbed and shiny as the furniture, and everyone is wearing new clothes. Hunger-teasing aromas float out of the steamy kitchen and fill the house, making it difficult to concentrate on other matters. But it is not yet time for the food.

The stage is set in the dining room for the ceremonial part of the meal. The woman of the house has covered the table with fine linen and lighted the candles as though in preparation for the Sabbath. Indeed, the holiday is considered a Sabbath, being designated a "holy convocation" in the Bible. But this is no ordinary table with ordinary place settings.

In a prominent place on the table sits the seder plate, the focal point of the whole seder service. This seder plate is a large, blue-enameled brass dish. It is specially designed, with divisions for each of the six symbolic foods, but a poor family may use an ordinary large serving plate

without partitions. The symbolic foods on the plate are much the same as those used on seder tables for the past several hundred years.

First we see on the plate the roasted shank bone of a lamb (or sometimes a chicken neck instead). The name of this symbol is *zeroah,* which means "arm," or, in animals, "shoulder." It represents the Paschal sacrifice, which is no longer possible. The *zeroah* also speaks of the outstretched arm of the Lord, by which He freed His people from Egypt.

Next we see a hard-boiled egg that has been roasted to a brown color. Its name on the seder plate is *baytzah,* which literally means "egg." However, the symbolic name for the egg is *haggigah,* meaning the holiday sacrifice that was made in Temple times. Many interpret this egg as a symbol of new life and hope and triumph over death (resurrection). Before the regular meal, hard-boiled eggs are sliced and given to all the persons at the table. They dip the eggs in salt water, which represents tears, and eat them to portray mourning over the destruction of the Temple.

The seder plate holds three kinds of bitter herbs. Two of these we recognize as being bitter. One, a piece of whole horseradish root,§ is called *chazereth* in Hebrew. The other is freshly ground horseradish, in Hebrew, *maror.* The third bitter herb, surprisingly, is a piece of lettuce, parsley or celery. It is designated *karpas,* and is the first food that will be eaten at the seder. The ancients considered lettuce and endive to be bitter herbs. The Talmud states: "Just as lettuce at first tastes sweet and then bitter, so did the Egyptians treat our ancestors . . . in Egypt. At first they settled them in the best part of the land, . . . but

§If horseradish is difficult to obtain, some people use a whole onion or a whole, large, white radish.

later they embittered their lives" (Yerushalmi Pesaḥim 29c). In the contemporary Passover service, the *karpas* is not usually considered a bitter herb. Rather, it is thought of as a symbol of life, because it is usually a green of some sort. However, Jewish people of some cultures do use radishes or raw potato instead. These substitutions remain in keeping with the ancient concept of using bitters for the first course.

Last on the seder plate we see a sweet, brownish mixture of chopped apples, nuts, raisins, cinnamon, and wine, called *charoseth*. Jewish people who come from Middle Eastern and Mediterranean cultures, where they do not grow apples but have an abundance of figs, use chopped figs instead of apples. Charoseth is symbolic of the mortar or red clay of Egypt, which the children of Israel used when they were forced to make bricks for Pharaoh. The question may be asked: If this mixture represents the bitter labor of Egypt, why is it sweet to the taste? "Ah," says one sage, "when we knew that our redemption drew nigh, even the bitterest of labor was sweet!" Charoseth is not commanded in Scripture. Nevertheless, like the eating of the hard-boiled eggs, it dates back to very ancient times.

In addition to the contents of the seder plate, three more items are essential to the Passover table: the unleavened bread, the wine, and the *Haggadah*.

The unleavened bread (*matzo*) of ancient times was flat, round, and irregular in shape. Likewise, the hand-baked matzo of today, used by very strict sects of Judaism, is round and somewhat irregular in shape. However, most modern matzo is machine-made and square, measuring about seven inches by seven inches. These flat, bland, crackerlike wafers are marked with even rows of tiny holes. The perforations, which are put in to prevent excessive

bubbling of the dough, cause uneven browning, which produces a striped appearance. In an earlier chapter we examined the symbolism of the unleavened bread as a type or picture of the sinless Messiah, Jesus.|| The appearance of the striped and pierced matzo brings to mind two verses of Scripture that help to complete the picture: "With his [Messiah's] *stripes* we are healed" (Isaiah 53:5, italics added), and "They [Israel] shall look upon me whom they have *pierced,* and they shall mourn for him" (Zechariah 12:10, italics added).

The unleavened bread on the table is encased in a special container called the *matzo tash.* The matzo tash is a square, white, silk bag that is divided into three compartments for three matzo wafers. If the family does not own one of these bags, three pieces of matzo must be stacked on a plate, each wafer separated with a napkin; then the three wafers are covered with another cloth. According to Jewish tradition, these three matzo wafers symbolize a unity. Contemporary Judaism gives no set interpretation of this unity, but there are several popular theories. One school of thought declares it to be the unity of the fathers—Abraham, Isaac, and Jacob; another thought is that the unity represents the unity of worship in Israel, that is, the priests, the Levites, and the rest of the congregation; a third idea is that it is the unity of crowns—the crown of learning, the crown of the priesthood, and the crown of kingship. Another Jewish source explains that two of the pieces of matzo represent the traditional loaves set out in the ancient Temple during the festival day, and the third is symbolic of Passover.# We shall explore yet another interpretation later in examining the ritual of the Passover seder.

||Chapter 3, p. 30.
#Herbert Bronstein, ed., *The New Union Haggadah,* rev. ed., p. 15.

Also at the seder table, beside each place setting, are small wine goblets—small because they will be filled with the sweet, red Passover wine four times during the seder. The custom of drinking four cups of wine dates back to ancient Temple times. The Mishnah teaches that, according to two authorities, Rabbi Yohanon and Rabbi Benayah, these four cups correspond to the four verbs in Exodus 6:6-7, describing God's redemption: I will *bring* you *out;* I will *deliver* you; I will *redeem* you; I will *take* you to be my people.

Two of the wine goblets at the table are usually larger and more ornate than the rest. This night they are silver, with intricate pictures of Bible history crafted into the metal. One of these goblets sits at the head of the table for the ruler of the feast; the other occupies a prominent place at the foot of the table, before an empty chair. It awaits the lips of Elijah, who, according to Malachi 4:5, is to announce the coming of the Messiah. The prophet is the invited guest of honor at every seder, for, should he come, it would indeed be the most festive of Passovers! The Messianic hope prevails more strongly at Passover than at any other time, for Midrashic tradition says: "Nisan is the month of redemption; in Nisan Israel was redeemed from Egypt; in Nisan Israel will again be redeemed" (Exodus Rabbah 15:12).**

The last item to notice on the table is a large, decorative book called the *Haggadah*. This book more than covers the host's dinner plate. Bound in a royal blue, velvety cover, it is inscribed with gold lettering and illustrated with many colorful reproductions of ancient art. Next to each person's place setting is a much smaller, plain, paper-

---

**Cf. chap. 6, pp. 53-55.

bound edition of the same book. The participants will need these to follow along during the service. The Haggadah not only tells what to do at the seder, but also when, how, and why. *Haggadah* is Hebrew for "telling," or "showing forth." It is the same root used in Exodus 13:8: "And thou shalt *shew* thy son in that day" (italics added). We find the same connotation in the Greek, where the apostle Paul, in describing the Last Supper, writes: "As often as ye eat this bread, and drink this cup, ye do *shew* the Lord's death till He comes" (1 Corinthians 11:26, italics added).

Our modern Haggadah is based on ancient writings in the Mishnah about Passover. These fragments date back to the second century. The first full record we have of the Haggadah is contained in a section of an old prayer book called *seder*, or *siddur*, which was edited in the ninth century by Rab Amram ben Sheshnah. The Haggadah finally emerged as a completely separate book in the thirteenth century. Much of the ritual and thought contained in even the latest versions goes back as far as Maccabean and second Temple times.

These, then, are all the unique foods and accouterments on the Passover table. But before the ritual meal itself is examined, there is yet another unusual feature to capture the attention. On each chair around the table there is a pillow. Most are sofa pillows, but often one or two bed pillows are used as well, for everyone must have one. Every person at the table tonight will recline or sit at ease during the ceremonial meal, for once we were slaves in Egypt, but now we are free. Once we ate the Passover in fear and haste, but tonight we eat in leisurely comfort and safety. We celebrate redemption. We rejoice in liberty!

8

The Modern Seder

In Jewish homes, the lighting of the holiday candles separates the sacred from the mundane, the Sabbath of rest from the week's cares. Tonight the blue white flames cast a halo of light over the holiday table, inspiring a sense of holiness. They lend a soft patina to the silver service, and their flickering glow is mirrored in the eyes of the seated company. Savory aromas from the kitchen mingle with the scent of the hot wax, the grapy smell of the wine, and the acrid fumes of freshly ground horseradish. An air of festivity reigns, tempered by solemn anticipation.

The father or grandfather of the family conducts the Passover seder. For this special occasion, the leader of the feast is wearing a long, white outer garment of cotton or silk called a *kitel*. The kitel is worn by Orthodox Jewish men at Passover and a few other special times. It is also a burial garment.* This wide-sleeved ceremonial robe is a symbol of purity, reminiscent of Temple times when no one could participate in the sacrifices unless he was in a state of Levitical purity. It also reminds us of the white robe of the high priest and of the robe of righteousness that God has promised to give to His elect (Isaiah 61:10; Revelation 6:11, 7:9). On his head, the leader of the feast wears a tall, white, silk head covering shaped like a crown, portraying

*See "Kitel," *Encyclopaedia Judaica,* 10:364.

In Jewish homes, the lighting of the holiday candles separates the sacred from the mundane, the Sabbath of rest
from the week's cares.

that on Passover night a man is king and religious leader over his own household.†

All eyes now turn expectantly to the leader as he stands and opens his Haggadah. He raises his wine glass for all to see and chants the *kiddush,* the prayer of sanctification that ushers in all Sabbath days and most of the Jewish holidays. This blessing expresses thanksgiving to God for choosing Israel and for giving feasts and holidays to His people. Tonight a special blessing is added for the commandment to commemorate the redemption from Egypt. The most widely recognized portion of this prayer is: "Blessed art thou, Lord our God, King of the Universe, Creator of the fruit of the vine." Upon the close of this benediction, everyone at the table sips from the first cup of wine, called the *cup of sanctification.* This cup of sanctification consecrates the ritual meal.

Next the hostess brings in a small towel and a silver bowl filled with water. This ceremonial washbasin contains only about a cup of water. The leader dips his fingertips into the bowl and dries them with the towel in preparation for handling the food. He picks up the *karpas* (celery, parsley, or lettuce) from the seder plate and hands a small portion to each participant. Everyone recites together: "Blessed art thou, Lord God, King of the Universe, who createst the fruit of the earth." And everyone dips the greens into salt water and eats. At ancient Greek and Roman banquets, this was the traditional beginning for a formal meal. This Hellenistic culture influenced Jewish custom and practices during the formative stages of stand-

---

†Jewish men wear a small head covering (*yarmulke*) when they pray. The miter described above is usually reserved for the cantor who leads the synagogue worship. At Passover the host, as religious leader of the evening, may wear the miter.

ardizing the seder. Contemporary thought endows the
ritual with added symbolism: the greens represent life,
which is often immersed in tears, represented by the salt
water.

The host now turns his attention to the *unity*, the three
wafers of unleavened bread. He bypasses the top wafer,
takes out the middle wafer, and breaks it in half. He puts
one of the halves back into the unity. Then he wraps the
remaining piece of this middle matzo in a white napkin
or puts it into a special, white, silk bag. While the children
cover their eyes, he hides or "buries" that portion of the
middle matzo, usually beneath one of the pillows or under
the tablecloth. This buried or hidden wafer of unleavened
bread now has a name, *aphikomen*. We will see the *aphikomen* later in the Passover service.

The ritual that follows is very old. We know this because the prayer is in Aramaic, the language used in the
land of Israel, mainly during the time of the second Temple. To this day it is read in Aramaic, not Hebrew. The
host uncovers the unleavened bread again, holds up the
plate, and everyone recites: "This is the Bread of Affliction
which our ancestors ate in the land of Egypt. Let all who
are hungry come and eat. Let all who are in need come
and celebrate Passover." Then they include phrases that
must have been added after the destruction of the Temple:
"This year we are here: next year in the land of Israel! This
year we are slaves: next year free men!" Here again, as
with the cup set out for Elijah, we see the Messianic hope
expressed. Although we are free from Egyptian slavery,
we are slaves. When the Lord brings us back to Zion in the
days of the Messiah, we will be truly redeemed, truly free!

Now the wine glasses are refilled, and the youngest child
at the table asks the traditional four questions:

Why is this night different from all other nights? On all other nights we can eat bread or matzo. Why, tonight, only matzo?

On all other nights, we can eat any kind of herbs. Why, tonight, bitter herbs?

On all other nights we don't dip herbs we eat into anything. Why, tonight, do we dip twice?

On all other nights we can eat either sitting up straight or reclining. Why, tonight, do we all recline?

The last question about reclining is a relatively late addition to the original questions. It may have been added as a replacement for the question referring to the Paschal lamb, which was asked while the Temple and the sacrifices remained: "Why do we eat only meat which is roasted?"

The father or grandfather replies with the prescribed answer in the Haggadah, taken from Deuteronomy 6:21 and 26:8: "We were Pharaoh's bondmen in Egypt; and the LORD our God brought us out thereof with a mighty hand and an outstretched arm." From this introductory statement proceeds the reading of the whole epic of redemption from the Haggadah. The Mishnah describes this answer as "beginning with shame and ending with glory" (Pesaḥim 10:4). The narrative combines Bible history and rabbinical commentary. It includes God's calling Abram out of idolatry, the hardships of the Hebrews in the land of Egypt, the punishment of the Egyptians, the dividing of the Red Sea, the giving of the Sabbath, and the giving of the Law. The climax is the recital of the ten plagues that God poured out on the Egyptians. With the mention of each plague, everyone dips or pours out one drop of wine from his wine goblet into a small saucer. This saucer, not

the goblet, is known as the cup. When the saucer is filled with the ten drops of wine, it is called *the cup of iniquity*, a term symbolic of God's judgments. Now is posed the rhetorical question: "Is it for this [the judgments] that we praise God?" The answer follows: "No, for God loved the Egyptians even as He loved us. But it is for God's infinite mercies that we praise Him."

This sets the stage for a happy song recounting the numerous acts of love and mercy that God bestowed upon Israel. The name of the song is one Hebrew word, *dayenu*, meaning, "it would have been sufficient." At the end of every line of the song comes the one-word refrain, "Dayenu," sung about ten times with much gaiety and handclapping. The song ends with the spoken words:

> Then how much more, doubled and re-doubled, is the claim the Omnipresent has upon our thankfulness! For He did take us out of Egypt and execute judgments . . . and justice . . . [did] tear the sea apart for us, . . . satisfy our needs in the desert, . . . give us the Sabbath [and] . . . the Torah [Law], . . . bring us into the land of Israel, and build us the House of His choosing to atone for all our sins.

Now, in obedience to the ancient admonition of Rabbi Gamaliel, the host makes special mention of the three crucial ingredients of the Passover: the Passover sacrifice (symbolized by the shank bone on the seder plate), the bitter herbs, and the unleavened bread (matzo). He explains each item, holding up the bitter herbs and matzo. However, he does not lift up the shank bone, lest what is only the symbol of the Passover lamb be given the significance of a real sacrifice, which is forbidden. Then he adds these words:

> In every generation let each man look on himself as if *he* came forth out of Egypt. As it is said: "And thou shalt tell thy son . . . it is because of what the Lord did for *me* when *I* came forth out of Egypt "[see Exodus 13:8].

This text is based on the teaching of the Mishnah (Pesaḥim 10:5) that the Exodus and redemption are not to be taken only as history; each Jew is to consider the experience as personal. (Even so, those of us who are spiritually redeemed by Jesus, the true Passover Lamb, see Him as being sacrificed for each of us, individually and personally, although the actual event happened two thousand years ago.)

Now the company raises the wine glasses in a toast of thanksgiving to the goodness of God and proclaims: "Let us then recite before Him a new song: Hallelujah!" They put the glasses down without drinking and recite Psalms 113 and 114, the first portion of the Hallel, which literally means "praise." Then they raise the wine glasses once again, repeating the ancient prayer of Rabbi Akiba, probably written just after the destruction of the Temple.

> Blessed art thou, O Lord, . . . who redeemed us . . . and has brought us to this night. . . . So, O Lord, . . . bring us to other festivals, . . . happy in the building of thy city. . . . And there may we eat of the sacrifices and the paschal offerings, whose blood will come unto the walls of thy altar for acceptance. Then shall we give thanks to thee with a new song, for our redemption and the liberation of our soul. Blessed art thou, O Lord, Redeemer of Israel. Blessed art thou, . . . Creator of the fruit of the vine.

This is the signal for drinking the second cup of wine, called the *cup of praise*.

Following the drinking of the second cup, they pass

around the basin of water. Everyone repeats the special prayer for ceremonial handwashing and washes his hands.

The head of the feast now breaks off pieces of unleavened bread and distributes them to all at the table. They recite together the prayers of thanksgiving for bread and for the commandment to eat unleavened bread; they eat a morsel of the matzo.

Next the host dips some of the bitter herb into the sweet charoseth mixture and offers a piece to each participant. Before eating it, they pronounce another benediction, thanking God for commanding the eating of bitter herbs. The resultant tears produced by this ceremony are a fitting memorial to the hardships of our ancestors!

The host goes on to make a sandwich of bitter herbs and unleavened bread. He eats it, saying:

> In memory of the Temple, according to the custom of Hillel. Thus did [Rabbi] Hillel when the Holy Temple still stood: he used to combine unleavened bread and bitter herbs and eat them together, to fulfill that which is said: "They shall eat it with unleavened bread and bitter herbs."

By this time, the younger children are a bit droopy-eyed from the warmth of the room, the sips of wine, and the hypnotic flickering of the candles. The older people are not drowsy; they have just been jolted into alertness by the mouthful of horseradish. But now the hostess sets aside the seder plate and disappears into the kitchen, and this is the real cue for everyone to come to life. Here come the good things that have been teasing their nostrils all day!

The Passover meal is literally a banquet. It usually begins with the traditional hard-boiled eggs dipped or flavored with salt water. Then come the appetizers. In Ash-

kenazi homes (those of northern and eastern European culture), two of the favorite appetizers are chopped liver, similar to the French liver pâté, and gefilte fish. The latter is similar to Scandinavian fish balls without the sauce. Jewish people like to use horseradish instead, even when it is not Passover. Then, almost always, there is a matzo ball soup, a rich, clear chicken broth accompanied by fluffy, featherlight dumplings made of finely ground matzo and many well-beaten eggs. The main course is usually a stuffed, roasted fowl, or beef of some kind. Jewish people today traditionally do not eat lamb on Passover, because there is no Temple and no Passover sacrifice. But those of us who are Jewish believers in the Messiah Jesus feel that it is fitting and meaningful to eat lamb at our Passover meals in remembrance of the One who came to be the Lamb, whose sacrifice overshadows the sacrifices of all the lambs slain in the Temple (Hebrews 9).

There are many more good things to eat, like salads and vegetables, limited only by the cook's imagination and resourcefulness. For dessert there are dried fruits, nuts, specially baked Passover cookies, sponge cakes, and coconut macaroons, all made without leaven; and imported marzipan and other candies from Israel.

Jewish people of Eastern and Mediterranean descent (Sephardim) have different favorite foods, in keeping with their own culture and tradition. Their cuisine often includes tomatoes, eggplant, and fruits like dates, figs, and oranges, which are native to their countries. The only foods never to be found on any Passover table, besides bread or other types of leaven, are pork and shellfish. These are forbidden at all times by Leviticus 11 and Deuteronomy 14 to those Jewish people who are still under the Law.

With dinner at an end, the dessert dishes are cleared

away, but the Passover seder is far from finished. Something is missing—the *aphikomen!* The name *aphikomen* comes from the Greek *epikomios,* meaning "after dinner revelry," or "that which comes last." In ancient times, this was apt to be rather rowdy. Since that type of behavior was totally unsuitable for a religious celebration, the rabbis of old substituted a solemn commemoration of the Paschal lamb. In Temple times, the lamb was the last thing to be eaten; now, in the absence of the sacrificial lamb, the unleavened bread was to represent the Passover sacrifice. The taste of the matzo and the memory of the lamb were to linger in the consciousness of each celebrant.

The children search now for the missiing *aphikomen,* making a little game of it. The adults call out advice as the children search the room: "You're way off base!" "You're cold." "You're getting warmer!" Soon someone finds it and turns it over to the head of the feast with a triumphant grin of anticipation, for he knows that he will receive a reward for it—a small gift or sum of money.

The gaiety and boisterousness of the search give way to solemnity as the ritual of the seder continues. The host unwraps the *aphikomen* and distributes olive-sized pieces to everyone.‡ All partake of it with quiet reverence. In Western culture, there is no blessing or word spoken. But in the Sephardic or Eastern tradition, they say: "In memory of the Passover sacrifice, eaten after one is sated." Nowhere do they add the prophetic words of Jesus at the Last Supper: "This is my body which is given for you" (Luke 22:19).

After this, no one may have any more food or drink at the seder other than the third and fourth cups of wine. At

‡By rabbinic tradition, an olive-sized morsel is the smallest over which one can say a blessing.

this point many Haggadahs include the recital of Psalm 126, one of the Songs of Ascent.

Now that the meal is officially concluded by the eating of the *aphikomen,* the ritual portion of the seder continues with the recitation of the final table grace. At Jewish meals there is a *berachah* (short prayer of thanks) for each food as it comes to the table, but the main table grace always comes after the meal. At the seder, the host now pours the third cup of wine before this prayer. Then he stands and repeats the traditional words in Hebrew: "Gentlemen, let us recite the blessing."

The seated company responds: "May the name of the Lord be blessed from now unto eternity."

The host continues: "Let us bless Him of whose food we have eaten."

Then the participants read a lengthy prayer of thanksgiving. Toward the end of this table grace, we hear again the expression of hope in God's final deliverance in the days of the Messiah.

> Take pity, O Lord, . . . on Israel, . . . on Zion the habitation of thy glory and on the kingdom of the House of David, thine anointed. . . . may there rise and come . . . the remembrance of us . . . and our fathers, and the remembrance of the Messiah the son of David, thy servant, . . . and Jerusalem thy holy city . . . and all thy people, the House of Israel, . . . on this festival. . . . The Compassionate One—may He send Elijah the prophet (may he be remembered for good) to us that he may bring us good tidings of salvations and consolations.

If Passover falls on a Friday night (the beginning of the Sabbath) they also add the following:

> The Compassionate One—may He cause us to inherit that

day which is all Sabbath and repose, in the everlasting
life. The Compassionate One—may He find us worthy of
the days of the Messiah and of the life of the world to
come.

This speaks of that ultimate Sabbath of rest about which
Paul is writing in Hebrews 4:9.

Immediately following that prayer, the host leads again
in the blessing over the wine, and everyone drinks the
third cup, commemorating the verse in Exodus 6:6b: "I
will redeem you with a stretched out arm." This third cup
is the *cup of redemption,* also at times called the *cup of
blessing.* It is the cup of redemption because, say the ancient commentaries, it represents the blood of the Paschal
lamb. Some Haggadahs call it the *cup of Elijah* because it
directly follows the prayer for the coming of Elijah.
Another reason for that title may be because of what hap-
pens next.

The children have been watching Elijah's cup at the
foot of the table. In some households, the cup was filled
at the beginning of the seder; in others, it is filled now.
They squint hard at the dark red contents of the cup. Will
Elijah come and drink from the cup? Maybe he is here
now, only he is invisible. Did he take a sip? It looks like
there is just a little less wine than there was a while ago!
Alas, if that is true, it is only due to evaporation. But maybe he is still going to come! Wait and see, but now we must
go on with the service.

Jewish scholars think the prayer that comes next, "Pour
out Thy Wrath," originated during the Middle Ages when
Jews were severely persecuted for the faith, especially at
Passover time. This prayer is not found in the earliest
editions of the Haggadah. It calls for God's judgment on
the heathen, and it sounds rather harsh. But taken in con-

text with the other prayers given above for the coming of
Elijah, it fits into the pattern of thought: "May God send
the Messiah, heralded by the prophet Elijah, to vanquish
all our enemies and set up His Kingdom of peace."

The leader now sends one of the children to open the
door to see if Elijah is coming in answer to the prayers.
The words are not prescribed until later in the Haggadah
reading, but just as the door is being opened, everyone
usually exclaims: "Blessed is he who cometh in the name
of the Lord!" The youngsters are round-eyed with awe as
the door slowly creaks open. A gust of cool night air
sweeps into the room, but no one is there. Oh well, maybe
next year! The child closes the door and comes back to the
table.

Next the host leads in the recitation of the second portion of the Hallel, Psalms 115 to 118. These verses are the
same as those of Temple times. They lead into the Great
Hallel, which is Psalm 136. In this well-known psalm, the
Levitical choir in the Temple sang out the praises of Jehovah and the great events of Israel's history. At the end
of each phrase or line, the congregation responded, "For
His kindness endureth forever!"

The earliest commentaries (Pesaḥim 10:7 of the Mishnah) record a "Benediction of Song" after the Hallel. The
Talmud, which is a commentary on the Mishnah, teaches
in Berakhot 59*b* that one of these benedictions was the
Great Hallel and another was at least some part of a hymn
called "The Breath of Every Living Thing." This closing
hymn before the fourth and final cup of wine is again a
prayer of praise and thanksgiving. It begins: "The breath
of every living thing shall bless Thy Name," and ends:
"Blessed art thou, O Lord, God and King, who art mightily

praised, God of thanksgivings, Lord of wonders, who chooses song and psalm, King, God, the life of the world."

Once again, everyone at the table lifts his wine glass and chants the blessing over wine. Everyone drinks from the fourth cup. This last cup of the Passover seder commemorates the verse in Exodus 6:7: "And I will take you to me for a people."

One of the modern versions of the Haggadah§ comments very aptly on the fourth cup and the verse it commemorates: "The redemption is not yet complete. The Fourth Cup recalls us to our covenant with the Eternal One, to the tasks that still await us as a people called to the service of God, to a great purpose for which the people of Israel live."

The editors of that particular Haggadah see the purpose of Israel as being "The preservation and affirmation of hope." But we, who are familiar with the promises and prophecies of Scripture, see a greater purpose for Israel— that of one day proclaiming to the whole world that the Messiah is, indeed, Saviour and King!

Because of the words, "I will take you to be my people," some call this fourth cup *the cup of acceptance.* Others prefer to call it *the cup of Elijah.* There is merit to both titles, for Elijah will yet come to herald the redemption that will be complete only when Israel fulfills God's entire plan; that is, when Israel recognizes and proclaims the Messiah (Zechariah 12:10), she will truly be the people of God, as foretold in Jeremiah 32:38-40.

And now, at last, with the drinking of the fourth cup, the seder is drawing to a close. Happy songs and festivity often continue afterward late into the night, but the service

§Herbert Bronstein, ed., *The New Union Haggadah*, rev. ed., p. 91.

officially ends with one last prayer for the rebuilding of Jerusalem:

> Concluded is the Passover seder,
> According to its law and custom.
> As we have lived to celebrate it,
> so may we live to celebrate it again.
> Pure One, who dwells in his habitation
> Redress the countless congregation.
> Speedily lead the offshoots of thy stock
> Redeemed, to Zion in joyous song.
> NEXT YEAR IN JERUSALEM!||

||Jewish people already living in Israel say instead: "Next year in Jerusalem *rebuilt!*"

9

The Fifth Question

The holiday candles have turned to shallow pools of wax in their festive holders; the savory meal is only a pleasant memory; and the children are losing their battle against heavy eyelids. The Haggadah is closed and returned to its place on the shelf for another year.

Once again we have rejoiced in the festival of freedom. We have made merry; we have been serious. We have feasted; we have taken the traditional four cups of wine; we have sung praises to God; we have rehearsed the story of His redemption of Israel. We have recalled His promises; we have discussed the comments of the ancient rabbis. We have heard the four questions, and we have learned what makes *this* night different from all other nights.

Still, other questions remain unanswered—unanswered because they go unasked. Elijah has not come. The naked bone on the Passover plate confronts us with the knowledge that we no longer have a Passover lamb, nor a Temple for the unified worship of Jehovah our God. Most of us are physically free from bondage, but are we not slaves to ourselves—our limitations, our faults, our circumstances? And then there is the ultimate question: Do those unanswered questions remain unanswered because we do not care enough to ask them, or because we are afraid to ask them?

In asking the four prescribed questions at the seder, the

little child knew just what to say. He had been rehearsing those lines for weeks. They rolled off his tongue in Hebrew or Yiddish as easily as his play songs, his name and address, the recitation of his schoolwork, so easily that he need not really think about what he was asking. But what if this same youngster were to become curious and interrupt the middle of the Passover service with: "Papa, why do you take out the middle piece of matzo instead of one of the others? Why do we hide the *aphikomen* and bring it back later?"

These are puzzling questions, for we have no one authoritative explanation of the symbolism of the unity of the three pieces of matzo on the Passover table. None of the given theories* about the nature of this unity provides a satisfactory answer to the hypothetical question, Why do we break the middle matzo?

If the unity is that of the three fathers, why do we break Isaac and not Abraham or Jacob? If it is the unity of worship, why do we break and hide the Levites rather than the priests or the congregation of Israel? Or if it is the three crowns, why do we single out the crown of the priesthood rather than the crown of learning or the crown of kingship? Why do we hide that middle wafer and bring it back later just before the third cup of wine?

Neither Jewish folklore nor rabbinical Judaism has an adequate answer to these perplexing questions. But there is a plausible explanation. Contemporary Jewish authorities readily admit that the Passover service and the Haggadah evolved through centuries of change, and some portions are older than others. One such Jewish author, Chaim Raphael, in his book *A Feast of History*, suggests that the rituals of the traditional seder "reflect in origin the world

*Cf. chapter 7, pp. 69 and 70.

in which the Jews found themselves while these ceremonies were being shaped for future generations."† Raphael acknowledges the influence of early Greek culture in the format of the Passover meal. He mentions obvious parallels between the symposia or dialogues of the Greek philosophers (Plutarch, Athanaeus, Macrobius, and Philo) and the ritual discussions of the Exodus by the ancient rabbis at the Passover seder. In another place in the same book, the author states:

> One has to assume a very fluid state of affairs . . . in the early centuries, even if we see an outline of the seder emerging in the Mishnah. The background of Jewish social life inside and outside Palestine was very unsettled because of political turmoil, the transition from statehood, the proliferation of sects, *and the ambivalent status for a time of the Jewish Christians.*‡

Admissions such as these by Jewish scholars lend credence to the thought that the many parallels between the entire ritual of the *aphikomen* and the corresponding symbolism found in the New Testament writings of the early Jewish Christians are too strong to be ignored.

Indeed, the status of the early Jewish Christians was, in the words of author Raphael, "ambivalent." They continued to worship in the Temple and attended the synagogue with their fellow Jews. For a while they were allowed, as a sect of Judaism, their differences of religious interpretation and emphasis, even as the Sadducees and Pharisees were allowed theirs. When the break finally came, the Jewish believers in Jesus did not abandon the synagogue. Rather, the synagogue expelled the Jewish Christians.

†Chaim Raphael, *A Feast of History,* p. 86.
‡Ibid., p. 95 (italics added).

Here, then, is the answer to the puzzling matter of the *aphikomen*. The early Jewish Christians incorporated into their own Passover services the spiritual lessons, customs, and insights taught them by Jesus Himself at the Last Supper. Because these early Jewish Christians at first were considered an acceptable sect of Judaism, some of their customs and interpretations became part of the Passover ritual of that time. The use of the *aphikomen* to commemorate the Passover lamb would have been particularly meaningful to the Jewish people after the destruction of the Temple, although after their break with the Jewish Christians the others might seek to deny the deeper significance of that broken matzo.

At the Last Supper, Jesus made that significance very clear when He instituted the new memorial to commemorate the sacrifice of Himself as the bread of life, the Lamb of God, the ultimate means of redemption for both Jews and Gentiles. Therefore, the words, "In memory of the Passover Lamb," spoken over the *aphikomen* in the Sephardic seder,§ present a double symbolism: The middle wafer *represents Jesus*, the Messiah, who, by His sinless, perfect life, *fulfilled the prophetic symbolism of the unleavened bread*, and who, by His sacrificial death, *fulfilled the prophetic symbolism of the Passover lamb!*

We see, then, in the three pieces of matzo on the Passover table, a truth that remains hidden from most of the Jewish community to this day. That truth of the unique unity of the eternal God is expressed in the *shemah*, the most widely spoken utterance of faith in all of Judaism, found in Deuteronomy 6:4: "Hear, O Israel: The Lord our

§Due to geographic factors, Sephardic culture and tradition (and even the pronunciation of the Hebrew language itself) bear the closest link to that Judaism that was practiced in the Holy Land before the final dispersion.

God is one LORD." In the original Hebrew, the word for
"one" is *echad*, meaning a composite oneness, rather than
the absolute number "one." This same word, *echad*, appears in Genesis 2:24 to signify that Adam and Eve became
"one flesh." It appears again in Ezekiel 37:16-19 to describe
the sign of the two sticks that became "one" in the prophet's hand. The three pieces of matzo, then, depict the eternal unity of God: the ineffable *Name*, who appeared to
Moses in the burning bush; the *Messiah*, the Son of David,
who became flesh to effect absolute redemption for the entire human race; and the *Holy Spirit*, who guides and
directs and empowers the redeemed of the Lord.

At the seder we single out the middle matzo, representing the Messiah, even as He was *foreordained* to die for
the sins of the whole world. We break the middle matzo,
signifying His *death*, for He was crucified, even as the
psalmist and the prophets foretold in Psalm 22, Isaiah 53,
and Daniel 9. We hide the middle matzo, signifying
burial. Just before the third cup of wine, perhaps symbol-
izing three days, we "resurrect" the middle matzo, just as
Jesus the Messiah *rose from the grave* in fulfillment of Job
19:25 and Psalm 16:10. Then all the faithful partake of
the middle matzo, signifying a personal, individual part in
the everlasting redemption of God, even as Jesus taught:

> I am the living bread which came down from heaven: if
> any man eat of this bread, he shall live for ever: and the
> bread that I will give is my flesh, which I will give for the
> life of the world (John 6:51).

That new memorial of the death, burial, and resurrection
of Jesus the Messiah symbolized the fulfillment of God's
plan for full redemption for all mankind, which plan was
foreshadowed in the first Passover observance. The Pass-

over celebration of redemption from Egypt still brings joy and gratitude to God's people. But truly blessed are those who appropriate by faith that new memorial, which speaks of the greater, eternal redemption of the soul.

As the Israelites were in bondage to Egypt and needed physical redemption, so all people are in bondage to sin and need to be forgiven and deemed the people of God. This broader redemption is available for all, whether Jews or Gentiles, who will trust in the atoning sacrifice of Messiah. But it is available *only* through the Messiah, Jesus. This is the redemption that brings true freedom from the bondage and hopelessness of sin and separation from a holy God.

Just as the redemption from Egypt foreshadowed the greater redemption to come, so many aspects of that earlier redemption portrayed another application in the lives of those redeemed of God through the blood of Jesus, the Lamb of God.

The Passover celebration reminded the children of Israel that once they were slaves to Pharaoh, but now they were free through the power of the Almighty. Those who are redeemed by Jesus, the Messiah, must remember that once they were slaves to sin, but now they are free from its power.

The slaying of the Passover lamb dramatically depicted to the children of Israel the cost of their rescue and redemption. Those who are redeemed by the death of Jesus the Messiah must remember the terrible cost of redemption—the agony and death of the perfect Lamb of God, who gave His life as an atonement for sin.

Then, in celebrating the Passover, the children of Israel remembered their journey in the wilderness. They recalled the victories Jehovah gave them over their enemies. They

remembered that He fed them with manna and gave them water that they might live; that He did not leave them to wander alone, but He led them by His very presence in a pillar of cloud by day and in a pillar of fire by darkest night; that He gave them rules to order their lives; that when willfulness and lack of faith led them to sin, He provided the brazen serpent for their healing and forgiveness; that He gave them a Sabbath of rest; and finally, that He brought them into the land flowing with milk and honey, which He had promised to the fathers.

For the eternally redeemed of God, life is a journey through the wilderness of the world. Yet the Lord gives us victory over the devil, the enemy of our souls. He feeds us with the bread of life and gives us springs of living water; He leads us in the way by the presence of His Holy Spirit, the Comforter who never leaves us. He writes His Law upon our hearts that we may live pleasing to Him; and if we stumble, He forgives our transgressions for Jesus' sake. He has given us the Sabbath of His rest, whereby we wear the robe of righteousness woven by the Messiah's sinless life, so that we need not struggle to achieve impossible standards by our own deeds. He promises us an eternal haven in the life to come in the city whose Builder and Maker is God.

Jehovah gave the Passover memorial to Israel to be a time of praise for past deliverance from Egypt and a time of renewing the hope for future and final deliverance. Those who would not keep the memorial (who wanted no part in the remembrance of God's merciful redemption) were cut off from the congregation. To be cut off from the congregation was not merely excommunication; it meant physical death.

The second, fuller redemption in God's Messiah does not threaten us with physical death if we should forget Him who gave His life for us. But putting aside that remembrance does cause the severance of fellowship with God and with His people, and neglecting to feed upon the broken Bread of Life starves the new life we have in Him. But if we confess our neglect and unfaithfulnes, He is faithful to forgive us and to cleanse us from all unrighteousness. Therefore, in the words of the apostle:

> Purge out therefore the old leaven, that ye may be a new lump, as ye are unleavened. For even Christ our passover is sacrificed for us: therefore let us keep the feast, not with old leaven, neither with the leaven of malice and wickedness; but with the unleavened bread of sincerity and truth (1 Corinthians 5:7-8).

Rejoice in the feast of the Lamb!

10

Come to the Feast

Blessed are they which are called unto the marriage supper of the Lamb (Revelation 19:9).

From the beginning of time, God has wanted to be more to man than most mortals would allow. He wants us to enter into the joy He has prepared for us, but we choose more temporal pleasures. He wants to be our cause for living, but we would rather live unto ourselves; He wants to be Lord, but we would rather be in command of our own lives. He wants us to trust Him, to rely on Him, and to know that He will do us good; but we are content to rely on the threadbare traditions of men rather than to obey His revelation of Himself.

It might be said: In the land of fools, a fool is crowned king. His reign is foolish, and the destiny of his people is to be fooled. Even so, among sinful men, people make themselves subjects of sin. Our best ways are rebellious and selfish; our best thoughts are corrupt. Our destiny is death, and both our lives and our deaths are but an infection on the face of the earth, itself accursed because of our impurity (Genesis 3:17; Romans 8:22).

The Israelites at Sinai trembled with their awareness of that impurity. Awed by the rumblings and fire on the holy

mountain, they insisted that Moses be a mediator between them and God (Exodus 20:19). Their dread to face God without a mediator was altogether appropriate, for a holy God cannot tolerate sinful man.

On that day of commandment at Mount Sinai, Jehovah instructed Moses: "Go down, charge the people, lest they break through unto the LORD *to gaze,* and many of them perish" (Exodus 19:21, italics added). No mortal can look upon God. Moses was highly favored of God, but He spoke even to Moses in a thick cloud that hid His glory. When Moses pleaded to see Him, he was told: "Thou canst not see my face: for there shall no man see me, and live" (Exodus 33:20). But the Lord in His mercy provided a way for Moses to behold Him and yet survive. He hid Moses in a cleft of rock in the holy mountain and allowed him to catch a fleeting view of His glory as He passed by.

The prophets of old, the best among men, were also highly favored of God. God appeared to them only in visions; yet when they glimpsed but a shadow of His being, they felt unworthy and undone. They were devastated, not because they faced an evil tyrant, but because they realized how sin-stained they were by the pollution of their earthly existence.

The prophet Isaiah, accounted the chief of the writing prophets, must have been one of the most righteous men of his time. But in the presence of God, he cried out in abject despair: "Woe is me! for I am undone; because I am a man of unclean lips, and I dwell in the midst of a people of unclean lips: for mine eyes have seen the King, the LORD of hosts" (Isaiah 6:5). His despair was not due to God's cruelty, but to the realization of how unrighteous his righteousness was. Later he wrote: "But we are all as an unclean thing, and all our righteousnesses are as filthy rags;

and we all do fade as a leaf; and our iniquities, like the wind, have taken us away" (Isaiah 64:6).

If the King of heaven were to allow us even a momentary view of Himself, we also would cringe in terror and despair. Our lives would become a tortured existence, and our deaths even worse, for we deserve eternal judgment. In His mercy, God does not reveal the infinite beauty of His holiness, lest we see the ugliness of our own sin and be destroyed by the consuming fire of His brightness.

In love, God does not show Himself to us, for we could not stand in His overwhelming presence. In compassion, He has allowed the separation caused by our sin; yet His heart aches with desire for our love.

God has provided a Mediator who spans the gap between our sinfulness and His holiness. Moses himself prophesied of this One who would come to Israel when he wrote in Deuteronomy 18:15-19:

> The LORD thy God will raise up unto thee a Prophet from the midst of thee, of thy brethren, like unto me; unto him ye shall hearken; according to all that thou desiredst of the LORD thy God in Horeb in the day of the assembly, saying, Let me not hear again the voice of the LORD my God, neither let me see this great fire any more, that I die not. And the LORD said unto me, They have well spoken that which they have spoken. I will raise them up a Prophet from among their brethren, like unto thee, and will put my words in his mouth; and he shall speak unto them all that I shall command him. And it shall come to pass, that whosoever will not hearken unto my words which he shall speak in my name, I will require it of him.

This Prophet to come would be like Moses in that He would be the Mediator between God and man. He would be the ultimate Prophet whom all must heed. Moses

spanned the gap between God and Israel for a short time, but he also was only mortal, with mortal flaws and the mortal destiny of death. Being mortal, he could not effect perfect, eternal mediation. In order for there to be perfect mediation, there needed to be some token or ground of eternal value. That Prophet to come was Jesus the Messiah, who alone was eligible to be the ground or token of mediation because He is eternal. (The Bible records in John 1:14 that "the Word was made flesh, and dwelt among us.")

By the sacrifice of Himself, Jesus the Messiah accomplished what neither Moses nor the sacrifices of bulls and goats could do. Not only was He the eternal Sacrifice; He was the eternal High Priest who offered that sacrifice. In this way, also, Jesus came as a Mediator like Moses. Even as Moses took a higher position than anyone in the Aaronic priesthood to intercede between the people and God, so the Messiah took precedence in His priesthood above the temporal role of the high priest in the Temple.

Jesus the Messiah is a Mediator whom we *can* gaze upon. Through Him, we *can* see God, our heavenly Father, for He said: "He that hath seen me hath seen the Father" (John 14:9*b*) and "I and my Father are one" (10:30). When we gaze upon Jesus, we see the love of God. Jesus is the cleft of the rock where we can hide from the consuming fire of God's holiness. From our vantage point in Him, we *can* see the glory of God as well as His love without being devastated.

We need not fear the righteous judgment of a holy God, for Jesus took upon Himself the wrath and judgment that rightfully are ours. We avoid God's devastating holiness by appropriating to ourselves the white robe of His righteousness to cover the nakedness of our sin. That robe of

righteousness is the only covering (*kiporah*) in which we may appear before God and not be consumed, and He yearns to give us that covering that cost Him so much.

Jesus the Messiah paid a terrible price that we might belong to God in love. Man finds it incomprehensible that God, the Creator, would desire an intimate relationship with His creation. Nevertheless, He does seek such a relationship with each member of the human race; He proposes a relationship that is even more personal than the marriage relationship.

God put into motion the restoration of His relationship with man through His people, Israel. He proposed to Abram in Ur. He betrothed Himself to Israel at the Passover, and He married the nation at Sinai. But Israel was no stronger in spiritual resoluteness than the rest of humanity around her. At times she strayed and became an unfaithful wife to Jehovah. Despite this, He looks upon her with compassion and love and has promised to restore her once again, and with her, all other nations who are willing. Therefore, when the Messiah of Israel came as the Word made flesh, He proposed that loving relationship with God to all humanity. He betrothed Himself to those who would believe and accept Him at Calvary. The consummation of that marriage is yet to take place when He returns for His beloved, the Bride called out from among believing Jews and Gentiles.

God constantly invites man! He entreated Abram to leave Ur and follow Him. He invited the children of Israel to share the feast of the Passover lamb, to leave Egypt and enter new life. But God invites us all to do more than merely move from one location to another. He invites man to become something *to* Him, something *for* Him. His

invitation is an honor bestowed in love, but it is also the offer of an opportunity we dare not refuse.

God has prepared a feast of redemption and joy to which all are invited. The invitation is for us to come to the marriage supper of the Lamb, to come and partake of Jesus, the bread of life, the Lamb of God, the Mediator who has taken our judgment upon Himself.

Come to the marriage supper of the Lamb! He is the holy Bridegroom. He seeks as His bride all those who will give themselves to Him in love; He is the holy Food that gives life and nourishment to the bride.

The Bible warns that everyone must deal with God's invitation. To those who will receive Him, Jesus is indeed the Lamb of God waiting to greet His beloved guests. But to those who spurn God's invitation of love, the Lamb will appear as the fierce Lion of the tribe of Judah. To those who ignore God's invitation, He will be a roaring Lion whose authority has been challenged.

Come to the feast of redemption and joy! God invites you. With ardor He entreats you to accept the relationship of love. You are the guest to be honored by accepting His offer of abundant life in Christ.

Come to the feast of the Lamb! Come to the feast that God is preparing for those who love Him. All you need to gain entrance is your wedding garment, His robe of righteousness.

The Lamb who was once slain lives again. He has gone to prepare a place for those who trust Him. He has promised to come again and take His beloved to celebrate the festival of joy, to live eternally in perfect union with Him.

Why not accept the invitation that God offers? You can do this by a simple prayer. Acknowledge that you cannot face God in His holiness, and that you need His robe of

righteousness; confess that Jesus is the Messiah, the Lamb of God who takes away the sin of the world; that He died to make atonement for your sins and lives again to be your Mediator. Tell God that you desire to follow Him in the newness of His resurrection life.

Then find a body of believers who regularly commemorate the event of His death. By baptism be identified with Him in that death, and be identified with His people in the newness of life that He gives. Even as that Passover table of long ago brought the ancient Israelites from slavery to freedom, come now to the table that brings new life!

In the words of the psalmist, taste and see that the Lord is good. Then you will find within your heart a melody to sing a new song with the redeemed of God—the song of Moses, the servant of God, and the song of the Lamb:

> Great and marvellous are thy works, Lord God Almighty; just and true are thy ways, thou King of saints. Who shall not fear thee, O Lord, and glorify thy name? for thou only art holy: for all nations shall come and worship before thee; for thy judgments are made manifest (Revelation 15:3-4).

This is the song that one day will reverberate throughout the courts of heaven at that ultimate feast of freedom and joy.

Come to God's feast!

> The Spirit and the Bride say, come. And let him that heareth say, come. And let him that is athirst come. And whosover will, let him take the water of life freely (Revelation 22:17).

A Final Note

The Jews for Jesus organization has prepared a Christ in the Passover demonstration, which is a sermonic presentation showing the accouterments and items used in the Passover seder. This presentation, along with the testimony of Hebrew Christians, is available for local churches. Anyone interested in having this program presented for his church or group should write:

Department of Mobile Evangelism
Jews for Jesus
60 Haight St.
San Francisco, California 94102

We are eager to help both Jews and Gentiles enter the salvation and joy that come through the Lamb of God. For more information or help with specific problems and questions, write to the above address, or to:

Moody Literature Ministries
820 North La Salle Drive
Chicago, Illinois 60610

Glossary

Abib (Aviv). Hebrew for the first month of the Jewish calendar, also called *Nisan.*

Akiba. A rabbi who lived at the time of the second Temple (died c. A.D. 133). He thought Bar Kochba was the Messiah.

Aliyah. Figuratively speaking, the "home going," when Jews make a return to the homeland (Israel). Literally, "the going up."

Aphikomen (Afikomen). Hebrew transliteration of Greek derivative, *epikomios.* That which comes last, the hidden Passover bread eaten at the seder.

Ashkenazim. Hebrew for a cultural branch of Judaism that developed in northern and eastern Europe and from which most American Jews are descended.

B'dikat Chametz. Hebrew for the formal search for leaven before Passover.

Berachah. Hebrew for a prayer of thanksgiving that always begins, "Blessed art Thou, O Lord, our God, King of the Universe." Literally, "a blessing" or "benediction."

Berakhot. Hebrew for a section of Talmudic commentary on benedictions.

Betzah. Hebrew for "egg," the symbolic hard-boiled and roasted egg on the seder plate; also called *Chaggigah* or *Haggigah.*

Booths, Feast of. In Hebrew, *Succoth,* the fifteenth day of the seventh month of the Jewish calendar; a seven-day holiday when Israel was to dwell in booths to commemorate the wilderness wanderings.

Breath of Every Living Thing, The. The closing hymn of the Passover seder.

Cantor. One who leads the chanting of prayers in the synagogue services.

Chametz (chometz). Hebrew for any fermented product of grain, all leavening agents; hence, that which makes "sour."

Charoseth. Hebrew for a mixture of apples, cinnamon, and nuts representing the mortar of Egypt; one of the symbolic foods on the seder plate.

Chazereth. Hebrew for a whole piece of, or a whole, bitter root, usually horseradish, on the seder plate.

Dayenu. Hebrew title of a Passover song meaning, "It Would Have Been Enough for Us."

Echad. Hebrew for "one."

Epikomios. Greek for after-dinner entertainment; that which comes after; basis for the word *aphikomen.*

Exodus Rabbah. A section of Talmudic commentary on the book of Exodus.

Feasts of Jehovah. The seven holidays that God commanded Israel to observe in Leviticus 23.

Firstfruits. A time of offering the first of the grain harvest to the Lord, observed on the second day of the Feast of Unleavened Bread.

Galatianism. A heresy that insisted that in order to be truly Christian, nonJews must be circumcised and obey the Law.

Gamaliel. A celebrated rabbi of the early part of the first century, the teacher of the apostle Paul.

Gefilte fish. Yiddish for fish balls or cakes made of ground fish, eggs, matzo meal, onions, and spices.

Gentile. Of or pertaining to any people who are not Jewish.

Great Hallel, The. Hebrew designation for Psalm 136.

Haggadah. Hebrew for the book that sets forth and explains the seder service.

Haggigah (Chaggigah). Hebrew for the festival offering; the other sacrifices offered in the Temple in addition to the Paschal lamb.

Hallel. Hebrew for "praise, a prayer of praise"; Psalms 113 to 118.

Hillel. A famous rabbi of the time of Herod, thought to be Gamaliel's grandfather.

Horeb. Another name for Mount Sinai, where God gave Israel His Law.

Hoshiah-na. Hebrew for English *Hosanna,* "please save."

Hyssop. A plant (perhaps the caper, *Capparis spinosa*) whose twigs were used in ceremonial sprinkling.

Judaize. To bring nonJews to accept the obligations of rabbinical tradition. *See* **Galatianism.**

Kal Hamira. An ancient Hebrew prayer spoken at the ritual cleansing of leaven.

Karpas. Hebrew for one of the symbolic foods on the seder plate, usually parsley or other greens.

Kiddush. Hebrew for a prayer of sanctification; the blessing over the ritual cup of wine.

Kiporah. Hebrew for "covering"; atonement that covers sin.

Kitel (Kittel). A long, white robe worn by Orthodox Jews at certain holidays and as a burial garment.

Levites. The tribe of Levi; the hereditary lineage from which came the priests and others who ministered in the Temple.

Lion of the tribe of Judah. A name for the Messiah, based on Revelation 5:5; cf. Isaiah 11:1.

Maror. Hebrew for bitter, ground horseradish, one of the symbolic foods on the seder plate.

Marzipan. A confection made of almond paste and sugar and molded into small shapes, usually of fruits and vegetables.

Matzo (Matzah). Hebrew for "without leaven"; a flat wafer of unleavened bread.

Matzo Tash. Yiddish for a baglike fabric container used for the three ritual wafers of unleavened bread at the seder.

Messiah. English translation of Hebrew *mashiach,* meaning the anointed One of God who was to come to fill all three offices for which one must receive anointing; prophet, priest, and king; the promised Redeemer.

Mishnah. Hebrew for the collection of oral law that forms the basis of the Talmud; compiled by Judah ha-Nasi (c. A.D. 135 to 220).

Mount Moriah. The Temple site at Jerusalem; also reputed to be the mountain where Abraham bound his son Isaac to the altar.

Mount Sinai. The mountain from which the Law was given by God to Moses.

Nisan. The first month in the Jewish calendar, also known as *Abib* or *Aviv*.

Orthodox. A modern term to distinguish traditional Jews from those who allow departure from tradition. Contemporary orthodoxy would be akin to ancient Phariseeism.

Pascha. Greek translation of the Hebrew *pesaḥ*, meaning "Passover."

Passover. From the Hebrew *pesaḥ;* the first of the seven feasts of Jehovah; the Paschal sacrifice; title may also include Feast of Unleavened Bread.

Pentecost. In Hebrew, *Shavuoth*, the Feast of Weeks; the fiftieth day after the first day of the Feast of Unleavened Bread; the festival of the ingathering of the firstfruits of the wheat harvest.

Pesaḥ. Hebrew for the holiday of Passover; the Paschal lamb.

Pesaḥim. Hebrew. A section of Talmudic commentary on the feast of the Passover.

Pharisees. A strict religious party who were known for their zealous adherence to the teaching of the rabbis concerning the Law. Their chief doctrine was that salvation and God's favor would come as a result of keeping the Law.

Priests. Descendants of Aaron (of the tribe of Levi) who officiated at religious services in the Temple; they also served as judges, physicians, and teachers.

Sadducees. An ancient sect of Judaism whose views and practices were opposed to those of the Pharisees. They denied

the authority of oral tradition, the resurrection of the dead, and the existence of angels.

Sanhedrin. The legislative and judicial parliament supposedly descendant from the seventy elders appointed by Moses.

Second Temple. The house of worship built at Jerusalem after the return of the Jews from the Babylonian Captivity.

Seder. Hebrew for "set order"; the ritual Passover meal which is observed in a specific order.

Seder plate. A shallow, usually compartmentalized dish that holds the symbolic foods of the Passover seder.

Sephardim. Hebrew for a cultural branch of Judaism; descendants of the Jews who fled Spain and Portugal after the Edict of Expulsion in 1492. They share a common language known as *Ladino* (a variant of Spanish), as opposed to northern European (Ashkenazi) Jews, who speak Yiddish (a Germanic dialect).

Shemah (Sh'ma). Hebrew for the most widely known Jewish confession of faith in one God; the first word of Deuteronomy 6:4, from which the prayer derives its name.

Siddur. Hebrew for the Jewish prayer book; the set order of prayers.

Talmud. The two commentaries on the Mishnah, one produced in the Holy Land about A.D. 275, the other in Babylonia about A.D. 500; the designation for both the Mishnah and the commentaries on it (*Gemara*).

Torah. Hebrew for the Pentateuch; the first five books of the Bible; the Law given to Moses; the scroll containing the first five books of the Bible, used in the synagogue.

Trumpets, Feast of. The modern *Rosh Ha-Shanah*, the first day of *Tishri*, the seventh month of the Jewish calendar, celebrated as the Jewish New Year.

Unleavened Bread, Feast of. The second of the seven feasts of Jehovah, which begins on the fifteenth of Nisan, directly after the Passover, and continues for seven days; a time when no leaven is to be eaten; also sometimes included in the festival

of Passover, whereby the two are designated as one holiday or festival lasting eight days.

Ur. An ancient Sumerian city and district in southern Babylonia by the Euphrates River; the home of Abraham.

Yarmulke. A skullcap worn by Orthodox Jews during prayers.

Yiddish. The language spoken by Jews of European ancestry; it is a dialect of old German.

Zeroah (Z'roah). Hebrew for "arm"; in animals, "shoulder"; the shank bone on the seder plate representative of the Paschal sacrifice (occasionally a chicken neck if a lamb shank is unobtainable).

Bibliography

Bronstein, Herbert, ed. *A Passover Haggadah*. Rev. ed. New York: Central Conference of American Rabbis, 1975.

Buksbazen, Victor. *The Gospel in the Feasts of Israel*. Philadelphia: Friends of Israel, 1954.

Edersheim, Alfred. *The Life and Times of Jesus the Messiah*. Grand Rapids: Eerdmans, 1962.

———. *The Temple, Its Ministry and Services as They Were at the Time of Jesus Christ*. Grand Rapids: Eerdmans, 1954.

Encyclopaedia Judaica. Jerusalem: Keter, 1971.

Encyclopedia Americana. New York: Americana Corp., 1966.

Glatzer, Nahum N. *The Passover Haggadah*. Rev. ed. New York: Schocken, 1953.

The Jewish Encyclopedia. New York: Funk & Wagnalls, 1901.

Levy, Isaac. *A Guide to Passover*. London: Jewish Chronicle Pubns., 1958.

Pink, A. W. *Gleanings in Exodus*. Chicago: Moody, n.d.

Raphael, Chaim. *A Feast of History*. New York: Simon & Schuster, 1972.

Regelson, A. *The Haggadah of Passover*. New York: Schulsinger, 1958.

Scharfstein, Ben-Ami. *Passover Haggadah*. New York: Shilo, 1959.

Index